Ivan Kushnir

Economy of Honduras

Series "Economy in countries"

first published: 2019
last updated: 2021-01-26

Ivan Kushnir. Economy of Honduras. Series "Economy in countries". - 2019. - 71 pages.

This book about the economy of Honduras from the 1970s to the 2010s. Source data from UN Data.

Size. In the 2010s, the GDP of Honduras was equal to $20.5 billion per year; the value of agriculture was $2.5 billion; the value of industry was $4.1 billion. Since the share in the world is between .01% and .1%, the country is classified as a small economy.

Productivity. In the 2010s, the GDP per capita was $2 272.4, the value of agriculture per capita was $278.8, the value of industry per capita was $458.9. Since the productivity is less the average below average, the economy is classified as least developed.

Growth. In the 2010s, the growth of GDP was 3.6%; the growth of agriculture was 4.4%; the growth of industry was 3.3%.

Structure. In the 2010s, the economy of Honduras included: services (36.0%), industry (20.8%), trade (17.5%), agriculture (12.7%), transportation (7.0%), and construction (6.0%).

Exports and imports. In the 2010s, the imports were 38.7% higher than the exports, the net imports were equal to 17.5% of the GDP. The technological structure of exports are not better than the structure of imports.

Consumption and reproduction. The attitude of reproduction to the consumption is not better than the global average, so the share of GDP in the world will not increase.

Series "Economy in countries": parallel.page.link/en

ISBN: 9781795168663

Contents

Part I. Size   4

   Chapter I. Gross domestic product   5

   Chapter II. Value added   9

   Chapter III. Gross national income   13

Part II. Structure   17

   Chapter IV. Agriculture   18

   Chapter V. Industry   22

      Chapter 5.1. Manufacturing   26

   Chapter VI. Construction   30

   Chapter VII. Transportation   34

   Chapter VIII. Trade   38

   Chapter IX. Services   42

Part III. External relations   46

   Chapter X. Exports   47

   Chapter XI. Imports   51

Part IV. Consumption   55

   Chapter XII. Government consumption expenditure   56

   Chapter XIII. Household consumption expenditure   60

   Chapter XIV. Food consumption   64

Part V. Reproduction   67

   Chapter XV. Gross fixed capital formation   68

Part I. Size

	The 2010s
GDP	$20.5 billion
The share in the world	0.026%
Share in the Americas	0.081%
Share in Central America	1.5%

Chapter I. Gross domestic product

The Honduran GDP rose from $1.5 billion per year in the 1970s to $20.5 billion per year in the 2010s, that is by $19.0 billion or 13.8 times. The change occurred at $14.4 billion due to a 3.3-fold increase in prices, as also at $1.8 billion due to a 1.4-fold increase in productivity, as well as at $2.8 billion due to the expansion in population. The average annual growth in GDP is 3.8%. The minimum value of GDP was in 1970 at $824.4 million. The maximum value of gross domestic product was in 2019 at $25.1 billion.

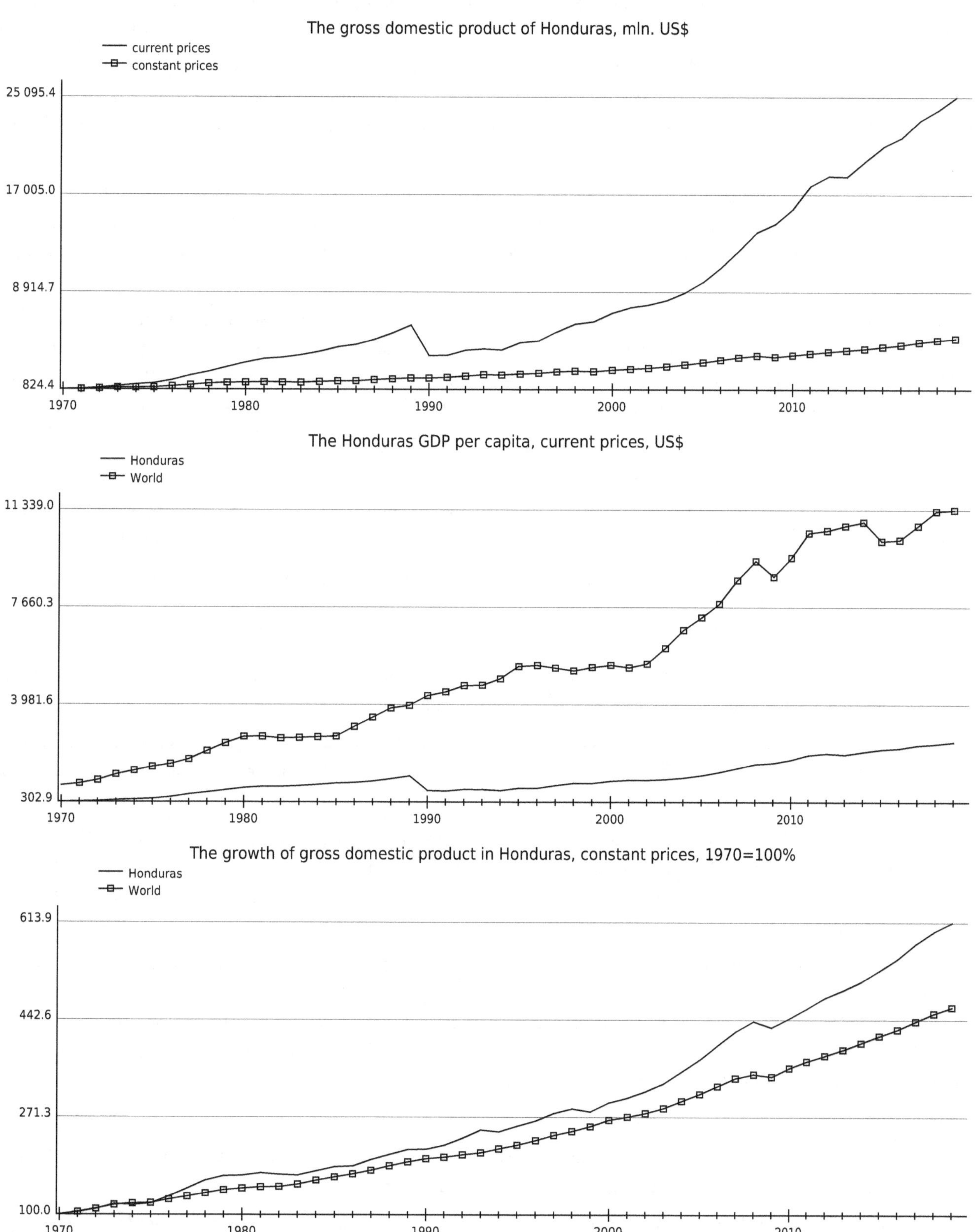

The 1970s

The Honduras GDP was $1.5 billion per year in the 1970s, ranked 103rd in the world. The share in the world was 0.023%, and 0.066% in the Americas.

The gross domestic product of Honduras consisted of: household consumption expenditure (70.7%), capital formation (20.8%), and government expenditure (12.5%).

The gross domestic product per capita in Honduras was $477.7 in the 1970s, ranked 131st in the world, and was on a par with Middle Africa ($479.8), Senegal ($473.8). The GDP per capita in Honduras was less than GDP per capita in the world ($1 620.8) in 3.4 times, and was less than GDP per capita in the Americas ($4 044.6) in 8.5 times.

The growth of gross domestic product in Honduras was 5.9% in the 1970s, ranked 57th in the world, and was on a par with Poland (5.9%). The growth of gross domestic product in Honduras (5.9%) was greater than growth of GDP in the world (4.1%), was greater than growth of GDP in the Americas (4.1%).

Comparison with neighbors. The gross domestic product of Honduras was greater than in El Salvador ($648.1 million); but less than in Guatemala ($3.4 billion) and in Nicaragua ($2.1 billion). The Honduran GDP per capita was greater than in El Salvador ($157.9); but less than in Nicaragua ($764.6) and in Guatemala ($527.2). The growth of GDP in Honduras was greater than in Guatemala (5.9%), in El Salvador (4.6%), and in Nicaragua (-0.014%).

Comparison with leaders. The Honduran GDP was less than in the USA ($1.7 trillion), in the USSR ($649.4 billion), in Japan ($558.0 billion), in Germany ($484.2 billion), and in France ($333.2 billion). The GDP per capita in Honduras was less than in the United States ($7.8 thousand), in France ($6.2 thousand), in Germany ($6.1 thousand), in Japan ($5.0 thousand), and in the USSR ($2.6 thousand). The growth of gross domestic product in Honduras was greater than in the USSR (4.8%), in Japan (4.6%), in France (3.9%), in the United States (3.5%), and in Germany (3.1%).

The 1980s

The Honduras gross domestic product was $4.3 billion per year in the 1980s, ranked 95th in the world, and was on a par with Brunei ($4.3 billion), Bahrain ($4.3 billion), Vietnam ($4.2 billion). The share in the world was 0.029%, and 0.080% in the Americas.

The GDP of Honduras consisted of: household consumption expenditure (72.3%), capital formation (16.5%), and public expenditure (14.5%).

The Honduran GDP per capita was $1 017.7 in the 1980s, ranked 118th in the world, and was on a par with Vanuatu ($1 017.9), Africa ($993.3), Tonga ($1 043.5). The Honduran gross domestic product per capita was less than GDP per capita in the world ($3 123.4) in 3.1 times, and was less than GDP per capita in the Americas ($8 168.9) in 8.0 times.

The growth of gross domestic product in Honduras was 2.5% in the 1980s, ranked 108th in the world, and was on a par with Europe (2.5%), the Seychelles (2.5%). The growth of gross domestic product in Honduras (2.5%) was less than growth of gross domestic product in the world (3.0%), was less than growth of GDP in the Americas (2.8%).

Comparison with neighbors. The GDP of Honduras was greater than in Nicaragua ($3.4 billion) and in El Salvador ($2.2 billion); but less than in Guatemala ($7.6 billion). The Honduran gross domestic product per capita was greater than in Guatemala ($933.0), in Nicaragua ($925.3), and in El Salvador ($444.9). The growth of GDP in Honduras was greater than in Guatemala (0.94%), in Nicaragua (-0.91%), and in El Salvador (-1.2%).

Comparison with leaders. The Honduran GDP was less than in the United States ($4.2 trillion), in Japan ($1.8 trillion), in Germany ($990.0 billion), in the USSR ($887.0 billion), and in France ($729.5 billion). The Honduran GDP per capita was less than in the USA ($17.4 thousand), in Japan ($15.0 thousand), in France ($12.9 thousand), in Germany ($12.7 thousand), and in the USSR ($3.2 thousand). The growth of GDP in Honduras was greater than in France (2.3%) and in Germany (1.9%); but less than in the USSR (4.3%), in Japan (4.3%), and in the United States (3.1%).

The 1990s

The GDP of Honduras was $4.8 billion per year in the 1990s, ranked 115th in the world, and was on a par with Guinea ($4.7 billion), Brunei ($4.8 billion). The share in the world was 0.017%, and 0.048% in the Americas.

The GDP of Honduras included: household consumption expenditure (65.9%), capital formation (28.5%), and public expenditure

(11.1%).

The gross domestic product per capita in Honduras was $843.2 in the 1990s, ranked 148th in the world, and was on a par with Ghana ($846.9), Georgia ($848.5), Africa ($833.3). The Honduran GDP per capita was less than gross domestic product per capita in the world ($5 020.1) in 6.0 times, and was less than GDP per capita in the Americas ($12 984.7) in 15.4 times.

The growth of GDP in Honduras was 2.7% in the 1990s, ranked 105th in the world, and was on a par with Austria (2.7%), Mauritania (2.7%), the Philippines (2.7%). The growth of gross domestic product in Honduras (2.7%) was less than growth of gross domestic product in the world (2.8%), was less than growth of GDP in the Americas (3.1%).

Comparison with neighbors. The gross domestic product of Honduras was greater than in Nicaragua ($4.1 billion); but less than in Guatemala ($12.1 billion) and in El Salvador ($8.1 billion). The gross domestic product per capita in Honduras was less than in El Salvador ($1 455.6), in Guatemala ($1 173.6), and in Nicaragua ($899.0). The growth of GDP in Honduras was less than in El Salvador (4.7%), in Guatemala (4.1%), and in Nicaragua (3.0%).

Comparison with leaders. The GDP of Honduras was less than in the United States ($7.6 trillion), in Japan ($4.3 trillion), in Germany ($2.2 trillion), in France ($1.4 trillion), and in the UK ($1.3 trillion). The gross domestic product per capita in Honduras was less than in Japan ($34.3 thousand), in the USA ($28.7 thousand), in Germany ($27.0 thousand), in France ($24.1 thousand), and in the UK ($22.9 thousand). The growth of GDP in Honduras was greater than in the United Kingdom (2.3%), in Germany (2.2%), in France (2.0%), and in Japan (1.5%); but less than in the USA (3.2%).

The 2000s

The gross domestic product of Honduras was $10.1 billion per year in the 2000s, ranked 113th in the world, and was on a par with Brunei ($10.0 billion). The share in the world was 0.022%, and 0.061% in the Americas.

The gross domestic product of Honduras consisted of: household expenditure (76.0%), capital formation (28.2%), and government consumption expenditure (15.9%).

The Honduran gross domestic product per capita was $1 374.9 in the 2000s, ranked 148th in the world. The Honduran gross domestic product per capita was less than GDP per capita in the world ($7 176.3) in 5.2 times, and was less than GDP per capita in the Americas ($19 020.5) in 13.8 times.

The growth of gross domestic product in Honduras was 4.3% in the 2000s, ranked 85th in the world, and was on a par with Thailand (4.3%), Tunisia (4.3%), Iran (4.3%). The growth of gross domestic product in Honduras (4.3%) was greater than growth of gross domestic product in the world (3.0%), was greater than growth of gross domestic product in the Americas (2.1%).

Comparison with neighbors. The Honduran gross domestic product was greater than in Nicaragua ($6.4 billion); but less than in Guatemala ($26.7 billion) and in El Salvador ($14.7 billion). The GDP per capita in Honduras was greater than in Nicaragua ($1 184.2); but less than in El Salvador ($2.4 thousand) and in Guatemala ($2.1 thousand). The growth of gross domestic product in Honduras was greater than in Guatemala (3.4%), in Nicaragua (2.9%), and in El Salvador (2.0%).

Comparison with leaders. The Honduras GDP was less than in the United States ($12.6 trillion), in Japan ($4.7 trillion), in Germany ($2.8 trillion), in China ($2.6 trillion), and in the United Kingdom ($2.3 trillion). The Honduran GDP per capita was less than in the USA ($42.8 thousand), in the UK ($38.4 thousand), in Japan ($36.4 thousand), in Germany ($34.0 thousand), and in China ($1 954.1). The growth of GDP in Honduras was greater than in the USA (1.9%), in the UK (1.7%), in Germany (0.73%), and in Japan (0.50%); but less than in China (10.3%).

The 2010s

The Honduras gross domestic product was $20.5 billion per year in the 2010s, ranked 111th in the world. The share in the world was 0.026%, and 0.081% in the Americas.

The gross domestic product of Honduras included: household expenditure (78.8%), capital formation (23.8%), and government consumption expenditure (14.9%).

The Honduras gross domestic product per capita was $2 272.4 in the 2010s, ranked 154th in the world, and was on a par with Moldova ($2.3 thousand). The Honduras gross domestic product per capita was less than gross domestic product per capita in the world ($10 603.1) in 4.7 times, and was less than gross domestic product per capita in the Americas ($26 129.9) in 11.5 times.

The growth of gross domestic product in Honduras was 3.6% in the 2010s, ranked 85th in the world, and was on a par with Nigeria (3.6%), Kosovo (3.6%), Costa Rica (3.6%). The growth of gross domestic product in Honduras (3.6%) was greater than growth of gross domestic product in the world (3.1%), was greater than growth of GDP in the Americas (2.2%).

Comparison with neighbors. The Honduran gross domestic product was 74.9% higher than in Nicaragua ($11.7 billion); but 2.9 times lower than in Guatemala ($59.8 billion) and 10.9% lower than in El Salvador ($23.0 billion). The gross domestic product per capita in Honduras was 19.8% higher than in Nicaragua ($1 897.5); but 38.8% lower than in Guatemala ($3.7 thousand) and 37.7% lower than in El Salvador ($3.7 thousand). The growth of gross domestic product in Honduras was greater than in Guatemala (3.5%), in Nicaragua (3.2%), and in El Salvador (2.1%).

Comparison with leaders. The Honduras gross domestic product was 874.9 times lower than in the USA ($18.0 trillion), 511.8 times lower than in China ($10.5 trillion), 254.7 times lower than in Japan ($5.2 trillion), 178.4 times lower than in Germany ($3.7 trillion), and 134.8 times lower than in the UK ($2.8 trillion). The Honduran gross domestic product per capita was 24.7 times lower than in the United States ($56.2 thousand), 19.7 times lower than in Germany ($44.7 thousand), 18.6 times lower than in the United Kingdom ($42.2 thousand), 18.0 times lower than in Japan ($40.9 thousand), and 3.3 times lower than in China ($7.5 thousand). The growth of gross domestic product in Honduras was greater than in the USA (2.3%), in Germany (1.9%), in the United Kingdom (1.8%), and in Japan (1.3%); but less than in China (7.7%).

Chapter II. Value added

The Honduras value added grew up from $1.5 billion per year in the 1970s to $19.9 billion per year in the 2010s, that is by $18.4 billion or 13.4 times. The change occurred at $13.0 billion due to a 2.9-fold increase in prices, as also at $2.6 billion due to a 1.6-fold increase in productivity, as well as at $2.8 billion due to the increase in population. The average annual growth in value added is 4.1%. The minimum value of value added was in 1970 at $820.9 million. The maximum value of value added was in 2019 at $24.0 billion.

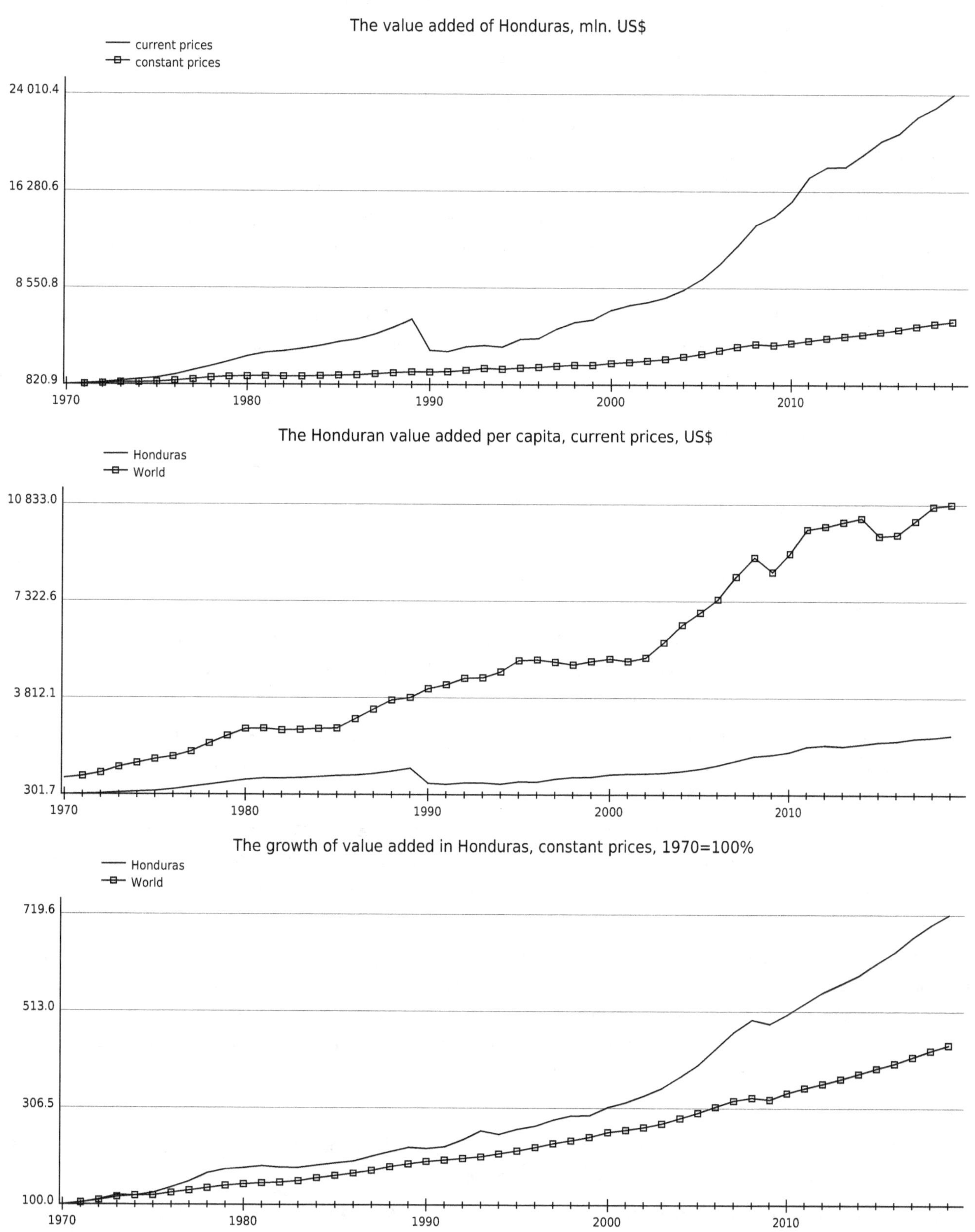

The 1970s

The value added of Honduras was $1.5 billion per year in the 1970s, ranked 103rd in the world, and was on a par with Brunei ($1.5 billion). The share in the world was 0.023%, and 0.066% in the Americas.

The total value added of Honduras consisted of: agriculture (26.4%), services (22.8%), industry (17.8%), trade (17.7%), transportation (9.5%), and construction (5.8%).

The Honduran value added per capita was $474.9 in the 1970s, ranked 129th in the world, and was on a par with Cameroon ($472.8), Middle Africa ($470.6), Dominica ($480.2). The Honduran value added per capita was less than value added per capita in the world ($1 564.4) in 3.3 times, and was less than value added per capita in the Americas ($3 985.3) in 8.4 times.

The growth of value added in Honduras was 6.4% in the 1970s, ranked 49th in the world, and was on a par with Greenland (6.4%), Yemen (6.4%), Grenada (6.5%). The growth of value added in Honduras (6.4%) was greater than growth of value added in the world (3.9%), was greater than growth of value added in the Americas (3.5%).

Comparison with neighbors. The value added of Honduras was less than in Guatemala ($3.1 billion), in Nicaragua ($2.1 billion), and in El Salvador ($1.6 billion). The value added per capita in Honduras was greater than in El Salvador ($399.6); but less than in Nicaragua ($754.4) and in Guatemala ($481.3). The growth of value added in Honduras was greater than in Guatemala (6.2%), in El Salvador (4.6%), and in Nicaragua (-1.6%).

Comparison with leaders. The Honduran value added was less than in the United States ($1.7 trillion), in the USSR ($649.4 billion), in Japan ($545.3 billion), in Germany ($444.9 billion), and in France ($297.3 billion). The value added per capita in Honduras was less than in the USA ($7.8 thousand), in Germany ($5.7 thousand), in France ($5.5 thousand), in Japan ($4.9 thousand), and in the USSR ($2.6 thousand). The growth of value added in Honduras was greater than in Japan (4.9%), in the USSR (4.8%), in France (3.7%), in Germany (3.1%), and in the USA (2.9%).

The 1980s

The value added of Honduras was $4.2 billion per year in the 1980s, ranked 97th in the world, and was on a par with Gabon ($4.3 billion), Brunei ($4.3 billion). The share in the world was 0.029%, and 0.079% in the Americas.

The total value added of Honduras included: services (29.3%), agriculture (19.9%), industry (17.9%), trade (17.0%), transportation (9.9%), and construction (6.0%).

The value added per capita in Honduras was $1 003.5 in the 1980s, ranked 117th in the world, and was on a par with Vanuatu ($1 018.4). The value added per capita in Honduras was less than value added per capita in the world ($3 029.9) in 3.0 times, and was less than value added per capita in the Americas ($8 159.2) in 8.1 times.

The growth of value added in Honduras was 2.4% in the 1980s, ranked 113th in the world, and was on a par with Namibia (2.4%), Switzerland (2.5%). The growth of value added in Honduras (2.4%) was less than growth of value added in the world (2.9%), was less than growth of value added in the Americas (2.7%).

Comparison with neighbors. The Honduran value added was greater than in El Salvador ($3.8 billion) and in Nicaragua ($3.2 billion); but less than in Guatemala ($7.0 billion). The Honduras value added per capita was greater than in Nicaragua ($863.8), in Guatemala ($857.3), and in El Salvador ($782.5). The growth of value added in Honduras was greater than in Guatemala (0.62%), in Nicaragua (-0.61%), and in El Salvador (-1.1%).

Comparison with leaders. The Honduras value added was less than in the USA ($4.2 trillion), in Japan ($1.8 trillion), in Germany ($907.0 billion), in the USSR ($887.0 billion), and in France ($650.9 billion). The value added per capita in Honduras was less than in the United States ($17.4 thousand), in Japan ($14.8 thousand), in Germany ($11.6 thousand), in France ($11.5 thousand), and in the USSR ($3.2 thousand). The growth of value added in Honduras was greater than in France (2.2%) and in Germany (2.0%); but less than in the USSR (4.3%), in Japan (4.2%), and in the United States (2.8%).

The 1990s

The value added of Honduras was $4.5 billion per year in the 1990s, ranked 115th in the world, and was on a par with Estonia ($4.4 billion). The share in the world was 0.016%, and 0.045% in the Americas.

The total value added of Honduras included: services (28.3%), industry (23.0%), agriculture (19.7%), trade (14.6%), transportation

(7.9%), and construction (6.4%).

The value added per capita in Honduras was $789.6 in the 1990s, ranked 148th in the world, and was on a par with Ivory Coast ($789.1), Africa ($793.2), Cameroon ($783.0). The value added per capita in Honduras was less than value added per capita in the world ($4 799.9) in 6.1 times, and was less than value added per capita in the Americas ($12 777.9) in 16.2 times.

The growth of value added in Honduras was 2.7% in the 1990s, ranked 106th in the world, and was on a par with Dominica (2.7%), the World (2.7%). The growth of value added in Honduras (2.7%) was less than growth of value added in the world (2.7%), was less than growth of value added in the Americas (2.8%).

Comparison with neighbors. The Honduran value added was greater than in Nicaragua ($3.7 billion); but less than in Guatemala ($11.2 billion) and in El Salvador ($7.5 billion). The Honduran value added per capita was less than in El Salvador ($1 345.4), in Guatemala ($1 083.5), and in Nicaragua ($808.2). The growth of value added in Honduras was less than in El Salvador (4.6%), in Guatemala (4.2%), and in Nicaragua (2.9%).

Comparison with leaders. The value added of Honduras was less than in the United States ($7.6 trillion), in Japan ($4.3 trillion), in Germany ($2.0 trillion), in France ($1.3 trillion), and in the United Kingdom ($1.2 trillion). The value added per capita in Honduras was less than in Japan ($34.2 thousand), in the USA ($28.6 thousand), in Germany ($24.5 thousand), in France ($21.6 thousand), and in the United Kingdom ($21.4 thousand). The growth of value added in Honduras was greater than in the United Kingdom (2.4%), in Germany (2.1%), in France (1.8%), and in Japan (1.8%); but less than in the United States (2.8%).

The 2000s

The value added of Honduras was $9.7 billion per year in the 2000s, ranked 111th in the world, and was on a par with Bosnia and Herzegovina ($9.6 billion). The share in the world was 0.022%, and 0.059% in the Americas.

The total value added of Honduras included: services (34.9%), industry (22.0%), trade (17.0%), agriculture (12.7%), transportation (7.4%), and construction (5.9%).

The value added per capita in Honduras was $1 317.4 in the 2000s, ranked 148th in the world, and was on a par with Sri Lanka ($1 319.1), the Philippines ($1 324.4), Nigeria ($1 293.0). The Honduran value added per capita was less than value added per capita in the world ($6 818.0) in 5.2 times, and was less than value added per capita in the Americas ($18 623.4) in 14.1 times.

The growth of value added in Honduras was 5.3% in the 2000s, ranked 44th in the world, and was on a par with Guyana (5.3%), Panama (5.3%). The growth of value added in Honduras (5.3%) was greater than growth of value added in the world (2.9%), was greater than growth of value added in the Americas (1.9%).

Comparison with neighbors. The Honduran value added was greater than in Nicaragua ($5.8 billion); but less than in Guatemala ($24.8 billion) and in El Salvador ($13.5 billion). The Honduras value added per capita was greater than in Nicaragua ($1 079.5); but less than in El Salvador ($2.2 thousand) and in Guatemala ($1 917.0). The growth of value added in Honduras was greater than in Guatemala (3.4%), in Nicaragua (3.2%), and in El Salvador (2.0%).

Comparison with leaders. The Honduran value added was less than in the United States ($12.6 trillion), in Japan ($4.7 trillion), in China ($2.6 trillion), in Germany ($2.5 trillion), and in the UK ($2.1 trillion). The value added per capita in Honduras was less than in the USA ($42.8 thousand), in Japan ($36.4 thousand), in the United Kingdom ($34.6 thousand), in Germany ($30.7 thousand), and in China ($1 954.1). The growth of value added in Honduras was greater than in the USA (1.7%), in the United Kingdom (1.7%), in Germany (0.65%), and in Japan (0.27%); but less than in China (10.2%).

The 2010s

The Honduran value added was $19.9 billion per year in the 2010s, ranked 111th in the world, and was on a par with Nepal ($19.9 billion), Papua New Guinea ($20.4 billion). The share in the world was 0.027%, and 0.080% in the Americas.

The total value added of Honduras included: services (36.0%), industry (20.8%), trade (17.5%), agriculture (12.7%), transportation (7.0%), and construction (6.0%).

The value added per capita in Honduras was $2 202.1 in the 2010s, ranked 154th in the world. The Honduras value added per capita was less than value added per capita in the world ($10 094.6) in 4.6 times, and was less than value added per capita in the Americas ($25 411.8) in 11.5 times.

The growth of value added in Honduras was 4% in the 2010s, ranked 73rd in the world. The growth of value added in Honduras (4.0%) was greater than growth of value added in the world (3.1%), was greater than growth of value added in the Americas (2.1%).

Comparison with neighbors. The value added of Honduras was 87.5% higher than in Nicaragua ($10.6 billion); but 2.8 times lower than in Guatemala ($56.2 billion) and 5.2% lower than in El Salvador ($21.0 billion). The Honduran value added per capita was 28.4% higher than in Nicaragua ($1 715.6); but 36.9% lower than in Guatemala ($3.5 thousand) and 33.7% lower than in El Salvador ($3.3 thousand). The growth of value added in Honduras was greater than in Guatemala (3.5%), in Nicaragua (3.3%), and in El Salvador (1.9%).

Comparison with leaders. The Honduras value added was 902.9 times lower than in the USA ($18.0 trillion), 528.1 times lower than in China ($10.5 trillion), 261.5 times lower than in Japan ($5.2 trillion), 166.0 times lower than in Germany ($3.3 trillion), and 124.2 times lower than in the UK ($2.5 trillion). The Honduras value added per capita was 25.5 times lower than in the USA ($56.2 thousand), 18.5 times lower than in Japan ($40.7 thousand), 18.3 times lower than in Germany ($40.3 thousand), 17.1 times lower than in the UK ($37.7 thousand), and 3.4 times lower than in China ($7.5 thousand). The growth of value added in Honduras was greater than in the United States (2.2%), in Germany (1.9%), in the United Kingdom (1.8%), and in Japan (1.3%); but less than in China (7.7%).

Chapter III. Gross national income

The GNI of Honduras enlarged from $1.4 billion per year in the 1970s to $19.1 billion per year in the 2010s, that is by $17.7 billion or 13.4 times. The change occurred at $13.4 billion due to a 3.3-fold increase in prices, as also at $1.6 billion due to a 1.4-fold increase in productivity, as well as at $2.7 billion due to the rise in population. The average annual growth in GNI is 3.7%. The minimum value of gross national income was in 1970 at $794.6 million. The maximum value of GNI was in 2019 at $23.2 billion.

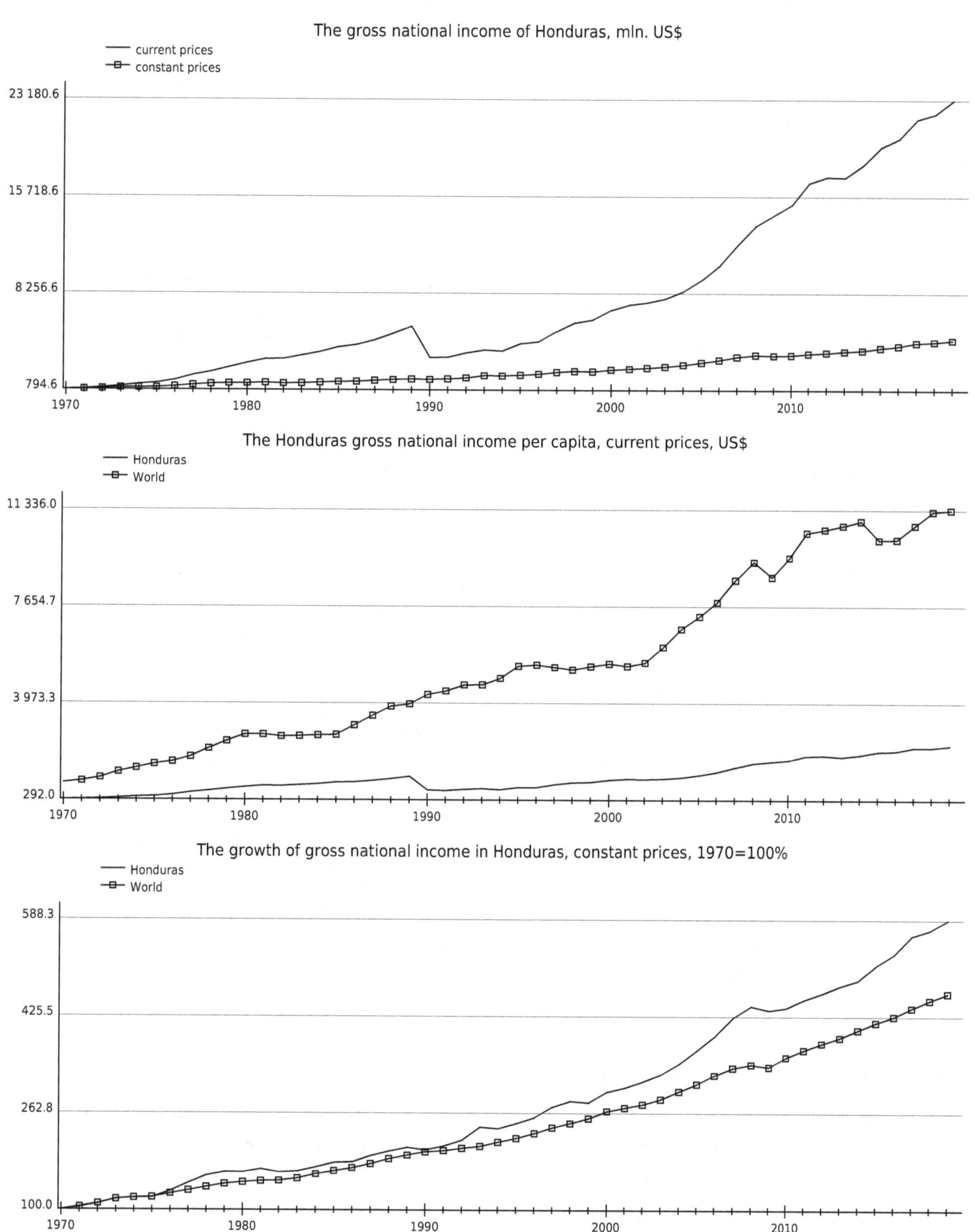

The gross national income of Honduras, mln. US$

The Honduras gross national income per capita, current prices, US$

The growth of gross national income in Honduras, constant prices, 1970=100%

The 1970s

The gross national income of Honduras was $1.4 billion per year in the 1970s, ranked 106th in the world, and was on a par with Nepal ($1.4 billion), Brunei ($1.4 billion), Jordan ($1.5 billion). The share in the world was 0.022%, and 0.063% in the Americas.

The gross national income per capita in Honduras was $456.4 in the 1970s, ranked 132nd in the world, and was on a par with Senegal ($463.1), Middle Africa ($463.7), Zambia ($446.2). The Honduran gross national income per capita was less than gross national income per capita in the world ($1 624.3) in 3.6 times, and was less than gross national income per capita in the Americas ($4 019.9) in 8.8 times.

The growth of gross national income in Honduras was 5.6% in the 1970s, ranked 63rd in the world, and was on a par with Israel (5.6%), French Polynesia (5.6%), Fiji (5.6%). The growth of gross national income in Honduras (5.6%) was greater than growth of GNI in the world (4.1%), was greater than growth of GNI in the Americas (4.0%).

Comparison with neighbors. The Honduras GNI was less than in Guatemala ($3.3 billion), in Nicaragua ($1.9 billion), and in El Salvador ($1.5 billion). The Honduras GNI per capita was greater than in El Salvador ($365.1); but less than in Nicaragua ($678.5) and in Guatemala ($521.0). The growth of gross national income in Honduras was greater than in El Salvador (4.7%) and in Nicaragua (-0.28%); but less than in Guatemala (6.1%).

Comparison with leaders. The GNI of Honduras was less than in the USA ($1.7 trillion), in the USSR ($649.4 billion), in Japan ($558.5 billion), in Germany ($486.2 billion), and in France ($334.3 billion). The Honduran GNI per capita was less than in the USA ($7.8 thousand), in France ($6.2 thousand), in Germany ($6.2 thousand), in Japan ($5.0 thousand), and in the USSR ($2.6 thousand). The growth of gross national income in Honduras was greater than in the USSR (4.8%), in Japan (4.7%), in France (3.9%), in the USA (3.5%), and in Germany (3.0%).

The 1980s

The Honduran GNI was $4.0 billion per year in the 1980s, ranked 96th in the world. The share in the world was 0.027%, and 0.075% in the Americas.

The Honduras GNI per capita was $949.0 in the 1980s, ranked 119th in the world, and was on a par with Eswatini ($949.4), Africa ($957.8), Papua New Guinea ($931.2). The Honduras gross national income per capita was less than GNI per capita in the world ($3 117.1) in 3.3 times, and was less than GNI per capita in the Americas ($8 063.2) in 8.5 times.

The growth of GNI in Honduras was 2.3% in the 1980s, ranked 108th in the world, and was on a par with Melanesia (2.3%), Northern Europe (2.3%), France (2.3%). The growth of gross national income in Honduras (2.3%) was less than growth of gross national income in the world (3.0%), was less than growth of GNI in the Americas (2.8%).

Comparison with neighbors. The GNI of Honduras was greater than in El Salvador ($3.4 billion) and in Nicaragua ($3.1 billion); but less than in Guatemala ($7.5 billion). The Honduran gross national income per capita was greater than in Guatemala ($914.3), in Nicaragua ($835.9), and in El Salvador ($702.4). The growth of GNI in Honduras was greater than in Guatemala (0.72%), in Nicaragua (-0.56%), and in El Salvador (-7.9%).

Comparison with leaders. The Honduran gross national income was less than in the United States ($4.2 trillion), in Japan ($1.8 trillion), in Germany ($996.5 billion), in the USSR ($887.0 billion), and in France ($732.1 billion). The GNI per capita in Honduras was less than in the USA ($17.4 thousand), in Japan ($15.0 thousand), in France ($13.0 thousand), in Germany ($12.8 thousand), and in the USSR ($3.2 thousand). The growth of gross national income in Honduras was greater than in Germany (2.0%); but less than in Japan (4.4%), in the USSR (4.3%), in the USA (3.1%), and in France (2.3%).

The 1990s

The gross national income of Honduras was $4.4 billion per year in the 1990s, ranked 117th in the world, and was on a par with Polynesia ($4.5 billion). The share in the world was 0.016%, and 0.045% in the Americas.

The GNI per capita in Honduras was $785.1 in the 1990s, ranked 148th in the world, and was on a par with Sri Lanka ($786.9), Senegal ($782.4), Cameroon ($778.3). The Honduran GNI per capita was less than gross national income per capita in the world ($4 991.4) in 6.4 times, and was less than GNI per capita in the Americas ($12 792.4) in 16.3 times.

The growth of GNI in Honduras was 3.2% in the 1990s, ranked 96th in the world, and was on a par with the Americas (3.2%). The growth of gross national income in Honduras (3.2%) was greater than growth of gross national income in the world (2.8%), was greater than growth of gross national income in the Americas (3.2%).

Comparison with neighbors. The Honduras GNI was greater than in Nicaragua ($3.8 billion); but less than in Guatemala ($11.9 billion) and in El Salvador ($7.3 billion). The GNI per capita in Honduras was less than in El Salvador ($1 305.6), in Guatemala ($1 159.6), and in Nicaragua ($822.8). The growth of gross national income in Honduras was greater than in El Salvador (2.5%); but less than in Guatemala (4.2%) and in Nicaragua (3.5%).

Comparison with leaders. The gross national income of Honduras was less than in the USA ($7.5 trillion), in Japan ($4.4 trillion), in Germany ($2.2 trillion), in France ($1.4 trillion), and in the United Kingdom ($1.3 trillion). The Honduran gross national income per capita was less than in Japan ($34.7 thousand), in the United States ($28.5 thousand), in Germany ($27.0 thousand), in France ($24.3 thousand), and in the United Kingdom ($23.0 thousand). The growth of gross national income in Honduras was greater than in France (2.2%), in the United Kingdom (2.0%), in Germany (2.0%), and in Japan (1.5%); but less than in the USA (3.4%).

The 2000s

The GNI of Honduras was $9.8 billion per year in the 2000s, ranked 114th in the world, and was on a par with the Bahamas ($9.5 billion), Brunei ($10.0 billion). The share in the world was 0.021%, and 0.059% in the Americas.

The Honduras gross national income per capita was $1 324.9 in the 2000s, ranked 150th in the world, and was on a par with East Timor ($1 341.5). The Honduran GNI per capita was less than gross national income per capita in the world ($7 165.2) in 5.4 times, and was less than gross national income per capita in the Americas ($18 970.5) in 14.3 times.

The growth of gross national income in Honduras was 4.5% in the 2000s, ranked 79th in the world, and was on a par with Slovakia (4.5%), Lebanon (4.5%), Ukraine (4.6%). The growth of GNI in Honduras (4.5%) was greater than growth of gross national income in the world (3.0%), was greater than growth of gross national income in the Americas (2.1%).

Comparison with neighbors. The gross national income of Honduras was greater than in Nicaragua ($6.2 billion); but less than in Guatemala ($26.2 billion) and in El Salvador ($14.1 billion). The gross national income per capita in Honduras was greater than in Nicaragua ($1 140.6); but less than in El Salvador ($2.3 thousand) and in Guatemala ($2.0 thousand). The growth of gross national income in Honduras was greater than in Guatemala (3.2%), in Nicaragua (3.1%), and in El Salvador (2.4%).

Comparison with leaders. The Honduras gross national income was less than in the United States ($12.7 trillion), in Japan ($4.8 trillion), in Germany ($2.8 trillion), in China ($2.6 trillion), and in the UK ($2.3 trillion). The gross national income per capita in Honduras was less than in the USA ($43.2 thousand), in the UK ($38.5 thousand), in Japan ($37.1 thousand), in Germany ($34.2 thousand), and in China ($1 950.5). The growth of GNI in Honduras was greater than in the United States (1.8%), in the United Kingdom (1.7%), in Germany (1.0%), and in Japan (0.62%); but less than in China (10.4%).

The 2010s

The Honduran GNI was $19.1 billion per year in the 2010s, ranked 111th in the world, and was on a par with Senegal ($19.0 billion). The share in the world was 0.025%, and 0.075% in the Americas.

The Honduran gross national income per capita was $2 117.2 in the 2010s, ranked 158th in the world, and was on a par with Uzbekistan ($2.2 thousand). The Honduras gross national income per capita was less than gross national income per capita in the world ($10 611.7) in 5.0 times, and was less than GNI per capita in the Americas ($26 262.7) in 12.4 times.

The growth of GNI in Honduras was 3% in the 2010s, ranked 107th in the world, and was on a par with Romania (3.0%), Somalia (3.0%), New Zealand (3.1%). The growth of GNI in Honduras (3.0%) was less than growth of GNI in the world (3.1%), was greater than growth of gross national income in the Americas (2.3%).

Comparison with neighbors. The Honduran gross national income was 67.3% higher than in Nicaragua ($11.4 billion); but 3.1 times lower than in Guatemala ($58.4 billion) and 13.0% lower than in El Salvador ($22.0 billion). The gross national income per capita in Honduras was 14.5% higher than in Nicaragua ($1 848.6); but 41.6% lower than in Guatemala ($3.6 thousand) and 39.2% lower than in El Salvador ($3.5 thousand). The growth of GNI in Honduras was greater than in El Salvador (1.9%); but less than in Guatemala (3.6%) and in Nicaragua (3.4%).

Comparison with leaders. The GNI of Honduras was 957.1 times lower than in the USA ($18.3 trillion), 547.3 times lower than in China ($10.5 trillion), 282.3 times lower than in Japan ($5.4 trillion), 196.0 times lower than in Germany ($3.7 trillion), and 143.6 times lower than in France ($2.7 trillion). The Honduras GNI per capita was 27.1 times lower than in the USA ($57.3 thousand), 21.6 times lower than in Germany ($45.8 thousand), 19.9 times lower than in Japan ($42.2 thousand), 19.6 times lower than in France ($41.4 thousand), and 3.5 times lower than in China ($7.5 thousand). The growth of GNI in Honduras was greater than in the USA (2.5%), in Germany (2.0%), in Japan (1.4%), and in France (1.4%); but less than in China (7.7%).

Part II. Structure

	The 2010s
agriculture	12.7%
industry	20.8%
construction	6.0%
trade	17.5%
transportation	7.0%
services	36.0%

Chapter IV. Agriculture

Agriculture, hunting, forestry, fishing (ISIC A-B)

The agriculture of Honduras grew up from $391.3 million per year in the 1970s to $2.5 billion per year in the 2010s, that is by $2.1 billion or 6.4 times. The change occurred at $1.2 billion due to a 1.9-fold increase in prices, as also at $164.7 million due to a 1.1-fold increase in productivity, as well as at $741.6 million due to the increase in population. The average annual growth in agriculture is 3.1%. The minimum value of agriculture was in 1970 at $234.0 million. The maximum value of agriculture was in 2017 at $2.9 billion.

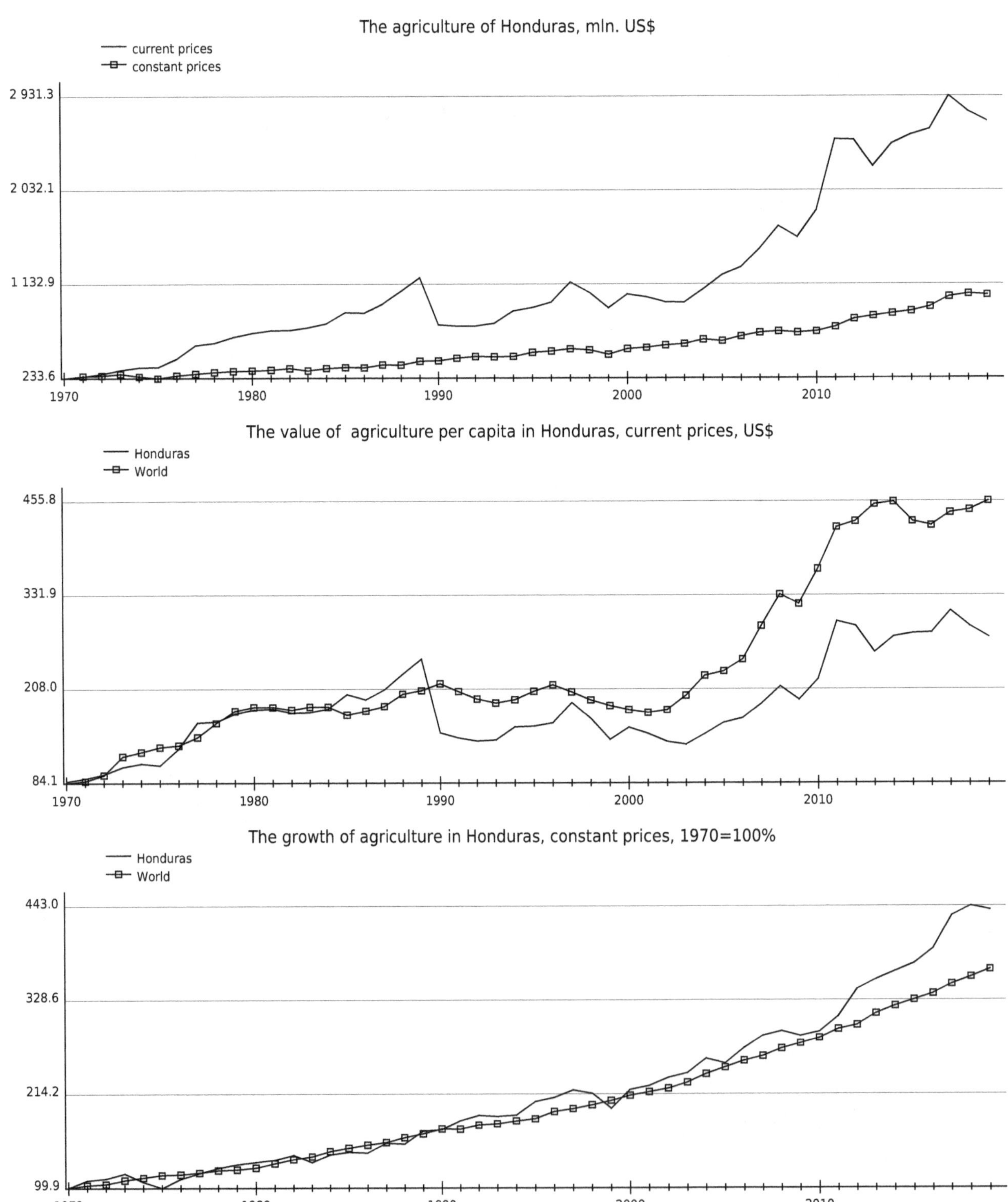

The agriculture of Honduras, mln. US$

The value of agriculture per capita in Honduras, current prices, US$

The growth of agriculture in Honduras, constant prices, 1970=100%

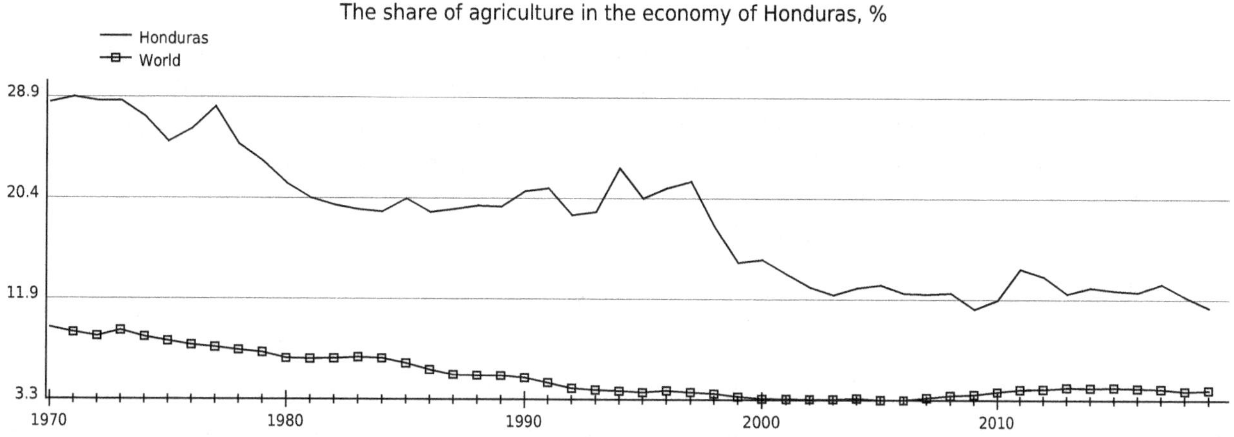

The 1970s

The Honduran agriculture was $391.3 million per year in the 1970s, ranked 90th in the world, and was on a par with Yemen ($393.6 million), Costa Rica ($382.9 million). The share in the world was 0.076%, and 0.44% in the Americas.

The share of agriculture in the economy of Honduras was 26.4% in the 1970s, ranked 48th in the world.

The sector of agriculture per capita in Honduras was $125.4 in the 1970s, ranked 75th in the world, and was on a par with the United Arab Emirates ($123.5), Samoa ($127.4), Barbados ($123.3). The value added of agriculture per capita in Honduras was less than agriculture per capita in the world ($127.6) by 1.7%, and was less than agriculture per capita in the Americas ($158.1) by 20.7%.

The growth of agriculture in Honduras was 2.8% in the 1970s, ranked 92nd in the world, and was on a par with Sri Lanka (2.8%), France (2.8%). The growth of agriculture in Honduras (2.8%) was greater than growth of agriculture in the world (2.2%), was greater than growth of agriculture in the Americas (1.9%).

Comparison with neighbors. The Honduran agriculture was greater than in Nicaragua ($302.9 million); but less than in Guatemala ($540.9 million) and in El Salvador ($463.4 million). The value added of agriculture per capita in Honduras was greater than in El Salvador ($112.9), in Nicaragua ($109.2), and in Guatemala ($85.1). The growth of agriculture in Honduras was greater than in Nicaragua (2.6%); but less than in Guatemala (5.0%) and in El Salvador (4.9%).

Comparison with leaders. The sector of agriculture in Honduras was less than in the USSR ($88.7 billion), in China ($49.5 billion), in the USA ($42.6 billion), in India ($36.0 billion), and in Japan ($25.8 billion). The Honduran agriculture per capita was greater than in India ($58.3) and in China ($54.2); but less than in the USSR ($351.8), in Japan ($231.3), and in the USA ($195.0). The growth of agriculture in Honduras was greater than in China (2.4%), in Japan (0.52%), in the USA (0.34%), and in India (0.30%); but less than in the USSR (7.0%).

The 1980s

The sector of agriculture in Honduras was $842.6 million per year in the 1980s, ranked 89th in the world, and was on a par with Rwanda ($850.0 million), Senegal ($826.5 million). The share in the world was 0.093%, and 0.54% in the Americas.

The share of agriculture in the economy of Honduras was 19.9% in the 1980s, ranked 58th in the world, and was on a par with Cabo Verde (19.8%), Indonesia (19.9%), Egypt (19.7%).

The value of agriculture per capita in Honduras was $199.2 in the 1980s, ranked 81st in the world, and was on a par with Central America ($199.3), Panama ($195.9). The sector of agriculture per capita in Honduras was greater than agriculture per capita in the world ($186.6) by 6.8%, and was less than agriculture per capita in the Americas ($237.6) by 16.2%.

The growth of agriculture in Honduras was 2.8% in the 1980s, ranked 76th in the world, and was on a par with the USSR (2.8%), Africa (2.8%), Dominica (2.8%). The growth of agriculture in Honduras (2.8%) was less than growth of agriculture in the world (3.1%), was greater than growth of agriculture in the Americas (2.6%).

Comparison with neighbors. The value added of agriculture in Honduras was greater than in El Salvador ($717.4 million) and in Nicaragua ($495.3 million); but less than in Guatemala ($1.2 billion). The value of agriculture per capita in Honduras was greater than in El Salvador ($146.4), in Guatemala ($143.2), and in Nicaragua ($134.5). The growth of agriculture in Honduras was greater than in

Guatemala (1.0%), in Nicaragua (-2.8%), and in El Salvador (-9.9%).

Comparison with leaders. The value of agriculture in Honduras was less than in the USSR ($125.8 billion), in China ($94.9 billion), in India ($70.4 billion), in the United States ($68.7 billion), and in Japan ($49.7 billion). The Honduran agriculture per capita was greater than in India ($90.7) and in China ($88.5); but less than in the USSR ($457.2), in Japan ($410.0), and in the USA ($286.8). The growth of agriculture in Honduras was greater than in the USSR (2.8%) and in Japan (0.41%); but less than in China (5.3%), in India (4.4%), and in the United States (3.7%).

The 1990s

The Honduran agriculture was $880.3 million per year in the 1990s, ranked 104th in the world. The share in the world was 0.077%, and 0.39% in the Americas.

The share of agriculture in the economy of Honduras was 19.7% in the 1990s, ranked 68th in the world.

The value of agriculture per capita in Honduras was $155.9 in the 1990s, ranked 126th in the world, and was on a par with Turkmenistan ($155.1), Kyrgyzstan ($155.0), Puerto Rico ($156.8). The agriculture per capita in Honduras was less than agriculture per capita in the world ($199.8) by 22.0%, and was less than agriculture per capita in the Americas ($288.9) by 46.1%.

The growth of agriculture in Honduras was 1.5% in the 1990s, ranked 113th in the world, and was on a par with Turkey (1.5%), Colombia (1.5%). The growth of agriculture in Honduras (1.5%) was less than growth of agriculture in the world (2.2%), was less than growth of agriculture in the Americas (2.4%).

Comparison with neighbors. The agriculture of Honduras was greater than in Nicaragua ($774.0 million); but less than in Guatemala ($1.8 billion) and in El Salvador ($927.7 million). The sector of agriculture per capita in Honduras was less than in Guatemala ($171.1), in Nicaragua ($168.4), and in El Salvador ($166.3). The growth of agriculture in Honduras was greater than in El Salvador (1.4%); but less than in Nicaragua (3.4%) and in Guatemala (3.0%).

Comparison with leaders. The Honduran agriculture was less than in China ($139.0 billion), in the USA ($96.1 billion), in India ($91.4 billion), in Japan ($78.9 billion), and in Brazil ($36.8 billion). The value added of agriculture per capita in Honduras was greater than in China ($112.7) and in India ($95.6); but less than in Japan ($625.5), in the USA ($363.4), and in Brazil ($228.7). The growth of agriculture in Honduras was greater than in Japan (-1.8%); but less than in China (4.3%), in Brazil (3.0%), in India (2.8%), and in the USA (2.6%).

The 2000s

The value of agriculture in Honduras was $1.2 billion per year in the 2000s, ranked 103rd in the world, and was on a par with Zambia ($1.2 billion). The share in the world was 0.079%, and 0.43% in the Americas.

The share of agriculture in the economy of Honduras was 12.7% in the 2000s, ranked 80th in the world, and was on a par with Northern Africa (12.7%), Fiji (12.7%).

The Honduran agriculture per capita was $166.7 in the 2000s, ranked 138th in the world, and was on a par with Pakistan ($167.7). The value added of agriculture per capita in Honduras was less than agriculture per capita in the world ($240.3) by 30.6%, and was less than agriculture per capita in the Americas ($327.5) by 49.1%.

The growth of agriculture in Honduras was 3.8% in the 2000s, ranked 49th in the world, and was on a par with the Dominican Republic (3.8%), Vietnam (3.8%). The growth of agriculture in Honduras (3.8%) was greater than growth of agriculture in the world (3.0%), was greater than growth of agriculture in the Americas (2.7%).

Comparison with neighbors. The agriculture of Honduras was greater than in Nicaragua ($1.0 billion) and in El Salvador ($943.0 million); but less than in Guatemala ($3.2 billion). The sector of agriculture per capita in Honduras was greater than in El Salvador ($156.3); but less than in Guatemala ($246.8) and in Nicaragua ($193.6). The growth of agriculture in Honduras was greater than in Guatemala (3.0%) and in El Salvador (0.21%); but less than in Nicaragua (4.2%).

Comparison with leaders. The agriculture of Honduras was less than in China ($297.7 billion), in India ($147.6 billion), in the USA ($122.5 billion), in Japan ($57.1 billion), and in Nigeria ($47.6 billion). The agriculture per capita in Honduras was greater than in India ($129.7); but less than in Japan ($445.6), in the USA ($416.9), in Nigeria ($346.4), and in China ($224.5). The growth of agriculture in Honduras was greater than in the United States (3.6%), in India (2.0%), and in Japan (-1.3%); but less than in Nigeria (10.1%) and in

China (4.0%).

The 2010s

The sector of agriculture in Honduras was $2.5 billion per year in the 2010s, ranked 98th in the world, and was on a par with Albania ($2.5 billion). The share in the world was 0.079%, and 0.52% in the Americas.

The share of agriculture in the economy of Honduras was 12.7% in the 2010s, ranked 72nd in the world, and was on a par with Moldova (12.8%), Northern Africa (12.8%).

The sector of agriculture per capita in Honduras was $278.8 in the 2010s, ranked 140th in the world, and was on a par with India ($279.1), Nauru ($279.5), Southern Asia ($280.8). The value added of agriculture per capita in Honduras was less than agriculture per capita in the world ($432.1) by 35.5%, and was less than agriculture per capita in the Americas ($498.8) by 44.1%.

The growth of agriculture in Honduras was 4.4% in the 2010s, ranked 36th in the world. The growth of agriculture in Honduras (4.4%) was greater than growth of agriculture in the world (2.9%), was greater than growth of agriculture in the Americas (2.2%).

Comparison with neighbors. The value of agriculture in Honduras was 32.5% higher than in Nicaragua ($1.9 billion) and 87.1% higher than in El Salvador ($1.3 billion); but 2.4 times lower than in Guatemala ($5.9 billion). The agriculture per capita in Honduras was 30.8% higher than in El Salvador ($213.2); but 24.5% lower than in Guatemala ($369.4) and 9.3% lower than in Nicaragua ($307.5). The growth of agriculture in Honduras was greater than in Guatemala (2.9%), in Nicaragua (2.4%), and in El Salvador (-0.67%).

Comparison with leaders. The Honduras agriculture was 351.9 times lower than in China ($886.2 billion), 144.3 times lower than in India ($363.4 billion), 71.6 times lower than in the USA ($180.3 billion), 49.3 times lower than in Indonesia ($124.1 billion), and 38.0 times lower than in Nigeria ($95.8 billion). The agriculture per capita in Honduras was 2.3 times lower than in China ($631.9), 2.0 times lower than in the United States ($564.3), 47.8% lower than in Nigeria ($534.6), 42.3% lower than in Indonesia ($483.6), and 0.12% lower than in India ($279.1). The growth of agriculture in Honduras was greater than in India (4.1%), in Indonesia (3.9%), in China (3.8%), in Nigeria (3.6%), and in the USA (2.0%).

Chapter V. Industry

Mining, Manufacturing, Utilities (ISIC C-E)

The value added of industry in Honduras grew from $263.6 million per year in the 1970s to $4.1 billion per year in the 2010s, that is by $3.9 billion or 15.7 times. The change occurred at $2.9 billion due to a 3.4-fold increase in prices, as also at $445.1 million due to a 1.6-fold increase in productivity, as well as at $499.7 million due to the increase in population. The average annual growth in industry is 4.2%. The minimum value of industry was in 1970 at $138.3 million. The maximum value of industry was in 2019 at $5.3 billion.

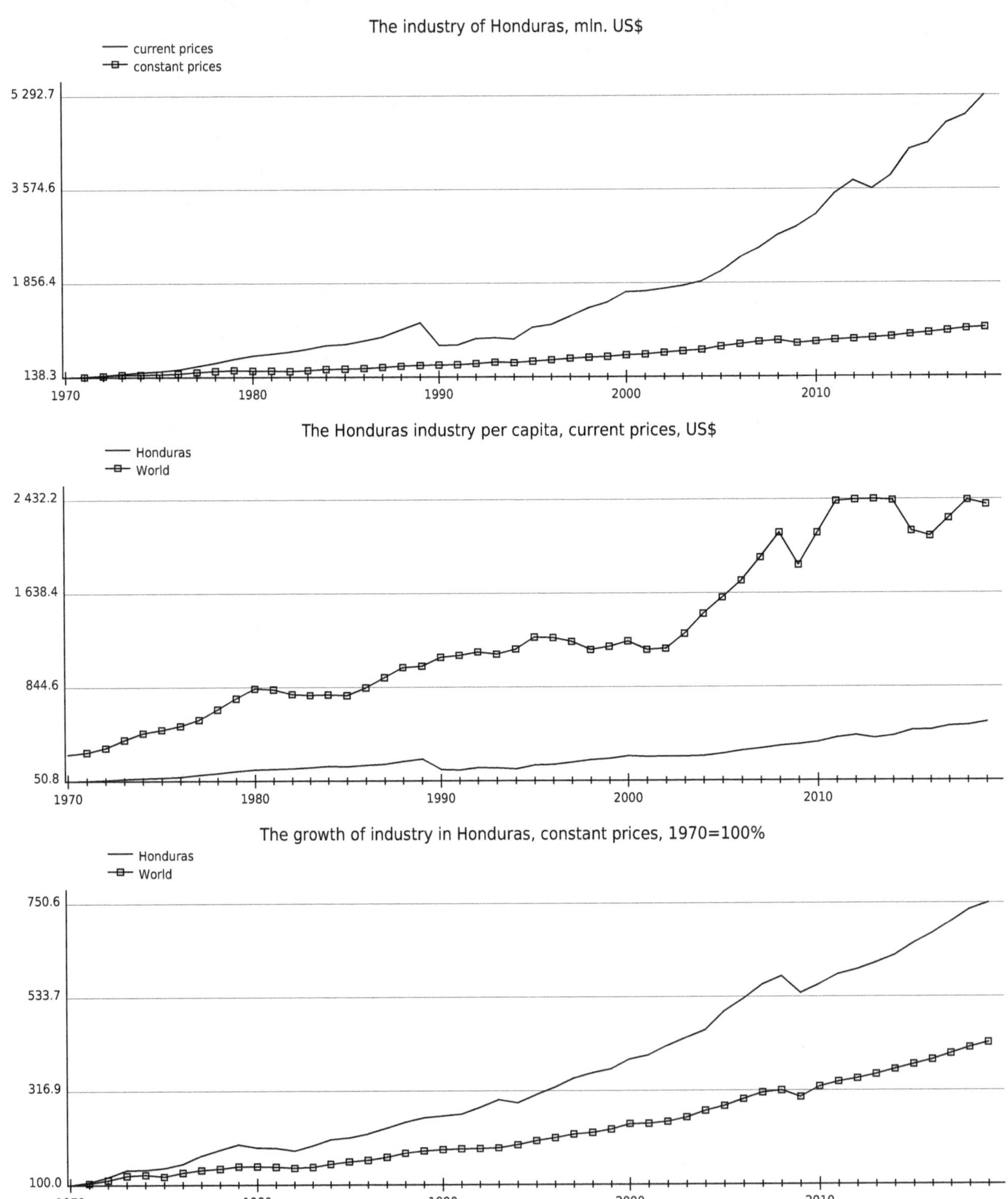

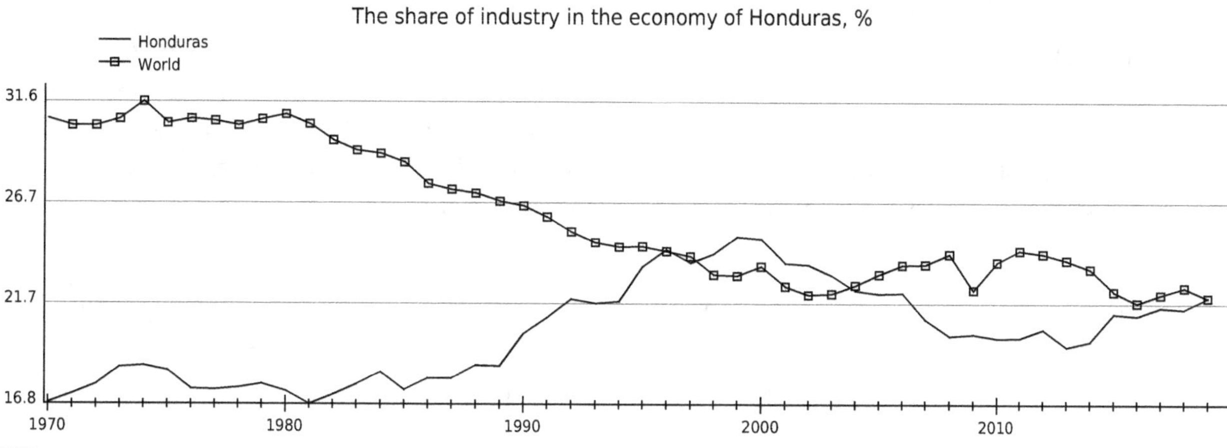

The 1970s

The sector of industry in Honduras was $263.6 million per year in the 1970s, ranked 108th in the world, and was on a par with Madagascar ($269.0 million). The share in the world was 0.014%, and 0.043% in the Americas.

The share of industry in the economy of Honduras was 17.8% in the 1970s, ranked 117th in the world, and was on a par with Niger (17.7%).

The industry per capita in Honduras was $84.5 in the 1970s, ranked 118th in the world, and was on a par with Kenya ($84.1), Samoa ($84.0). The Honduras industry per capita was less than industry per capita in the world ($480.5) in 5.7 times, and was less than industry per capita in the Americas ($1 091.1) in 12.9 times.

The growth of industry in Honduras was 7.6% in the 1970s, ranked 39th in the world, and was on a par with DPRK (7.6%), Bahrain (7.7%). The growth of industry in Honduras (7.6%) was greater than growth of industry in the world (4.0%), was greater than growth of industry in the Americas (3.2%).

Comparison with neighbors. The Honduras industry was less than in Guatemala ($685.7 million), in Nicaragua ($403.6 million), and in El Salvador ($285.7 million). The industry per capita in Honduras was greater than in El Salvador ($69.6); but less than in Nicaragua ($145.5) and in Guatemala ($107.9). The growth of industry in Honduras was greater than in Guatemala (6.8%), in El Salvador (2.9%), and in Nicaragua (-2.7%).

Comparison with leaders. The industry of Honduras was less than in the USA ($450.4 billion), in the USSR ($248.8 billion), in Japan ($185.6 billion), in Germany ($158.4 billion), and in the United Kingdom ($72.6 billion). The value added of industry per capita in Honduras was less than in the USA ($2.1 thousand), in Germany ($2.0 thousand), in Japan ($1 666.5), in the UK ($1 295.1), and in the USSR ($986.6). The growth of industry in Honduras was greater than in the USSR (5.2%), in Japan (4.5%), in the United States (2.4%), in Germany (2.1%), and in the UK (1.9%).

The 1980s

The Honduras industry was $761.8 million per year in the 1980s, ranked 99th in the world. The share in the world was 0.018%, and 0.055% in the Americas.

The share of industry in the economy of Honduras was 17.9% in the 1980s, ranked 116th in the world.

The industry per capita in Honduras was $180.1 in the 1980s, ranked 116th in the world, and was on a par with Bolivia ($181.7), Indonesia ($182.6), Anguilla ($177.4). The value of industry per capita in Honduras was less than industry per capita in the world ($861.8) in 4.8 times, and was less than industry per capita in the Americas ($2 085.6) in 11.6 times.

The growth of industry in Honduras was 2.8% in the 1980s, ranked 95th in the world, and was on a par with DPRK (2.8%). The growth of industry in Honduras (2.8%) was greater than growth of industry in the world (2.3%), was greater than growth of industry in the Americas (1.9%).

Comparison with neighbors. The Honduran industry was greater than in Nicaragua ($720.9 million) and in El Salvador ($676.2 million); but less than in Guatemala ($1.6 billion). The sector of industry per capita in Honduras was greater than in El Salvador ($138.0); but less than in Nicaragua ($195.8) and in Guatemala ($192.4). The growth of industry in Honduras was greater than in Guatemala

(0.47%), in El Salvador (0.098%), and in Nicaragua (-1.4%).

Comparison with leaders. The value of industry in Honduras was less than in the USA ($1.0 trillion), in Japan ($566.4 billion), in the USSR ($305.7 billion), in Germany ($297.5 billion), and in the United Kingdom ($171.2 billion). The value of industry per capita in Honduras was less than in Japan ($4.7 thousand), in the United States ($4.2 thousand), in Germany ($3.8 thousand), in the United Kingdom ($3.0 thousand), and in the USSR ($1 110.8). The growth of industry in Honduras was greater than in the USA (1.9%), in the UK (1.4%), and in Germany (1.2%); but less than in the USSR (5.3%) and in Japan (4.2%).

The 1990s

The sector of industry in Honduras was $1.0 billion per year in the 1990s, ranked 113th in the world, and was on a par with Congo ($1.0 billion), Cyprus ($1.0 billion), Guinea ($1.1 billion). The share in the world was 0.015%, and 0.049% in the Americas.

The share of industry in the economy of Honduras was 23.0% in the 1990s, ranked 92nd in the world, and was on a par with the CAR (23.0%), Central Asia (23.0%), El Salvador (23.1%).

The industry per capita in Honduras was $181.8 in the 1990s, ranked 141st in the world, and was on a par with DPRK ($179.9), Cameroon ($178.3). The Honduras industry per capita was less than industry per capita in the world ($1 175.6) in 6.5 times, and was less than industry per capita in the Americas ($2 704.1) in 14.9 times.

The growth of industry in Honduras was 3.7% in the 1990s, ranked 78th in the world, and was on a par with Oman (3.7%). The growth of industry in Honduras (3.7%) was greater than growth of industry in the world (2.5%), was greater than growth of industry in the Americas (2.8%).

Comparison with neighbors. The industry of Honduras was greater than in Nicaragua ($623.7 million); but less than in Guatemala ($2.3 billion) and in El Salvador ($1.7 billion). The value added of industry per capita in Honduras was greater than in Nicaragua ($135.7); but less than in El Salvador ($310.2) and in Guatemala ($225.8). The growth of industry in Honduras was greater than in Nicaragua (3.3%); but less than in El Salvador (7.4%) and in Guatemala (3.9%).

Comparison with leaders. The sector of industry in Honduras was less than in the United States ($1.5 trillion), in Japan ($1.2 trillion), in Germany ($534.0 billion), in China ($285.9 billion), and in the United Kingdom ($268.6 billion). The Honduran industry per capita was less than in Japan ($9.4 thousand), in Germany ($6.6 thousand), in the USA ($5.7 thousand), in the United Kingdom ($4.6 thousand), and in China ($231.9). The growth of industry in Honduras was greater than in the USA (2.8%), in Japan (1.3%), in the United Kingdom (1.2%), and in Germany (0.33%); but less than in China (13.1%).

The 2000s

The industry of Honduras was $2.1 billion per year in the 2000s, ranked 110th in the world. The share in the world was 0.021%, and 0.069% in the Americas.

The share of industry in the economy of Honduras was 22.0% in the 2000s, ranked 94th in the world, and was on a par with Switzerland (21.9%), Bulgaria (21.9%).

The industry per capita in Honduras was $289.4 in the 2000s, ranked 146th in the world, and was on a par with Nigeria ($295.0). The value of industry per capita in Honduras was less than industry per capita in the world ($1 573.8) in 5.4 times, and was less than industry per capita in the Americas ($3 499.5) in 12.1 times.

The growth of industry in Honduras was 4% in the 2000s, ranked 69th in the world, and was on a par with Eastern Europe (4.0%), Estonia (4.0%), Bosnia and Herzegovina (4.0%). The growth of industry in Honduras (4.0%) was greater than growth of industry in the world (2.9%), was greater than growth of industry in the Americas (1.4%).

Comparison with neighbors. The industry of Honduras was greater than in Nicaragua ($1.0 billion); but less than in Guatemala ($4.9 billion) and in El Salvador ($3.1 billion). The value added of industry per capita in Honduras was greater than in Nicaragua ($190.9); but less than in El Salvador ($508.0) and in Guatemala ($374.8). The growth of industry in Honduras was greater than in Nicaragua (3.5%), in Guatemala (2.4%), and in El Salvador (0.88%).

Comparison with leaders. The Honduras industry was less than in the USA ($2.1 trillion), in Japan ($1.1 trillion), in China ($1.1 trillion), in Germany ($629.4 billion), and in the UK ($345.1 billion). The value of industry per capita in Honduras was less than in Japan ($8.8 thousand), in Germany ($7.7 thousand), in the USA ($7.1 thousand), in the United Kingdom ($5.7 thousand), and in China ($795.3).

The growth of industry in Honduras was greater than in the USA (1.5%), in Germany (0.19%), in Japan (0.15%), and in the United Kingdom (-1.1%); but less than in China (11.1%).

The 2010s

The Honduran industry was $4.1 billion per year in the 2010s, ranked 112th in the world, and was on a par with Senegal ($4.2 billion), Latvia ($4.2 billion). The share in the world was 0.024%, and 0.098% in the Americas.

The share of industry in the economy of Honduras was 20.8% in the 2010s, ranked 99th in the world, and was on a par with Kosovo (20.8%), Melanesia (20.7%), Nigeria (20.9%).

The Honduran industry per capita was $458.9 in the 2010s, ranked 147th in the world. The value of industry per capita in Honduras was less than industry per capita in the world ($2 320.9) in 5.1 times, and was less than industry per capita in the Americas ($4 354.8) in 9.5 times.

The growth of industry in Honduras was 3.3% in the 2010s, ranked 86th in the world, and was on a par with Vanuatu (3.3%), Western Africa (3.3%), Burundi (3.3%). The growth of industry in Honduras (3.3%) was less than growth of industry in the world (3.5%), was greater than growth of industry in the Americas (1.8%).

Comparison with neighbors. The value of industry in Honduras was 76.4% higher than in Nicaragua ($2.3 billion); but 2.6 times lower than in Guatemala ($10.6 billion) and 11.5% lower than in El Salvador ($4.7 billion). The industry per capita in Honduras was 20.8% higher than in Nicaragua ($380.0); but 38.2% lower than in El Salvador ($741.9) and 30.5% lower than in Guatemala ($660.3). The growth of industry in Honduras was greater than in Guatemala (3.0%) and in El Salvador (1.9%); but less than in Nicaragua (5.7%).

Comparison with leaders. The Honduran industry was 888.5 times lower than in China ($3.7 trillion), 661.4 times lower than in the United States ($2.7 trillion), 287.2 times lower than in Japan ($1.2 trillion), 202.6 times lower than in Germany ($840.0 billion), and 107.0 times lower than in India ($443.4 billion). The industry per capita in Honduras was 34.7% higher than in India ($340.6); but 22.4 times lower than in Germany ($10.3 thousand), 20.3 times lower than in Japan ($9.3 thousand), 18.7 times lower than in the USA ($8.6 thousand), and 5.7 times lower than in China ($2.6 thousand). The growth of industry in Honduras was greater than in Germany (3.2%), in Japan (2.6%), and in the USA (2.2%); but less than in China (7.5%) and in India (6.5%).

Chapter 5.1. Manufacturing

(ISIC D)

The manufacturing of Honduras rose from $245.0 million per year in the 1970s to $3.5 billion per year in the 2010s, that is by $3.3 billion or 14.3 times. The change occurred at $2.4 billion due to a 3.3-fold increase in prices, as also at $347.5 million due to a 1.5-fold increase in productivity, as well as at $464.4 million due to the increase in population. The average annual growth in manufacturing is 4.1%. The minimum value of manufacturing was in 1970 at $128.9 million. The maximum value of manufacturing was in 2019 at $4.1 billion.

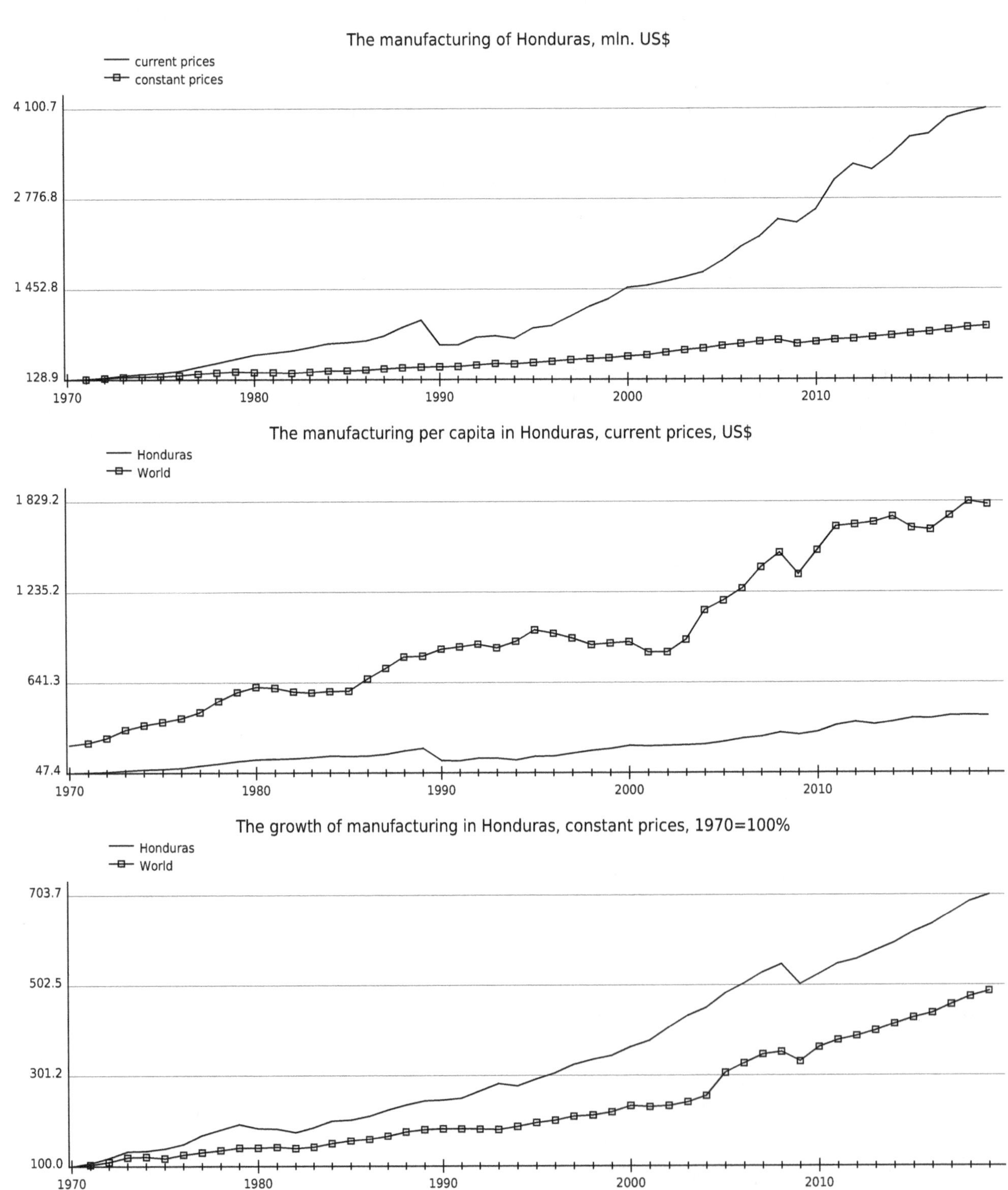

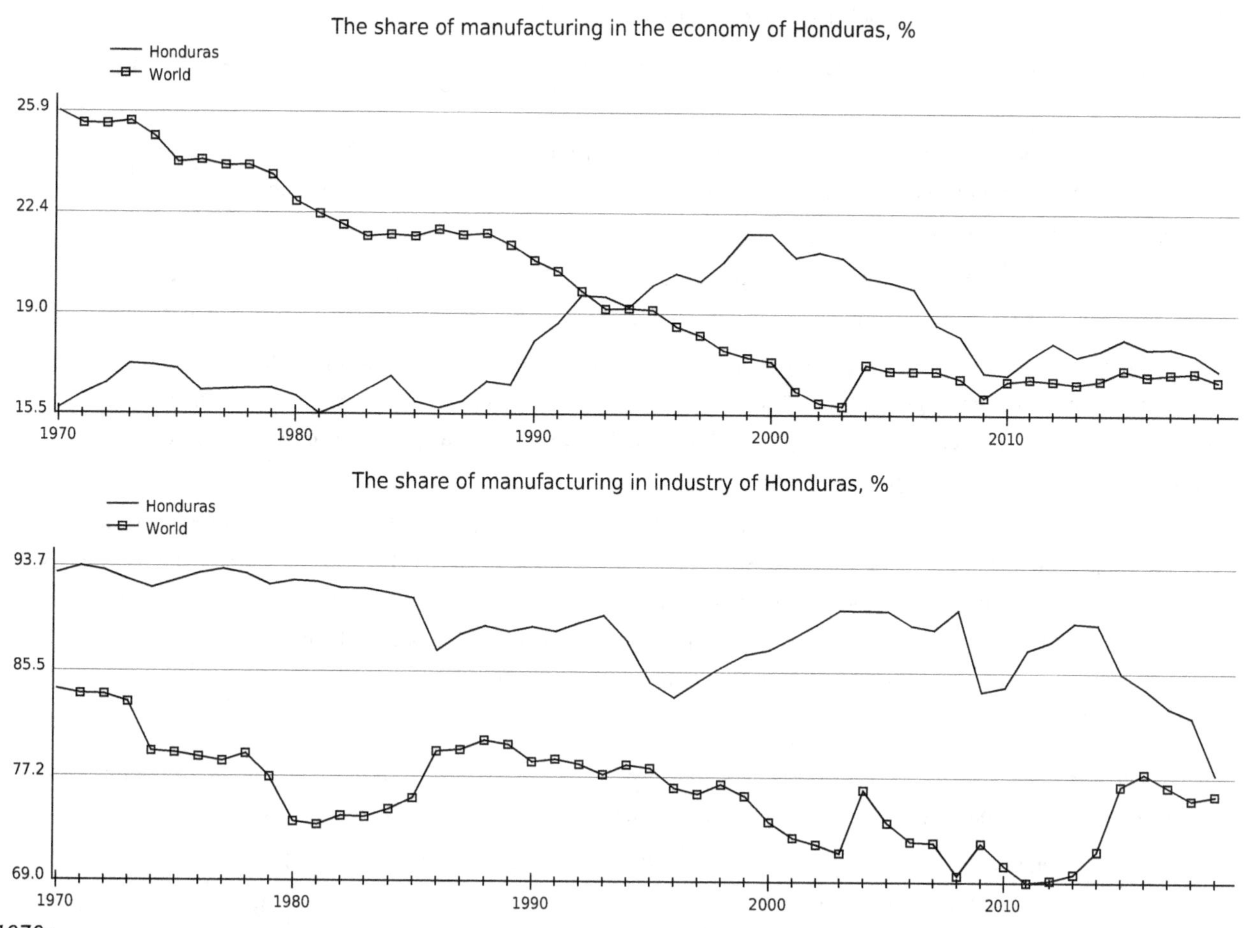

The 1970s

The sector of manufacturing in Honduras was $245.0 million per year in the 1970s, ranked 98th in the world, and was on a par with Iceland ($249.8 million). The share in the world was 0.016%, and 0.049% in the Americas.

The share of manufacturing in the economy of Honduras was 16.5% in the 1970s, ranked 79th in the world, and was on a par with Ireland (16.6%), Eastern Africa (16.5%).

The Honduran manufacturing per capita was $78.5 in the 1970s, ranked 102nd in the world, and was on a par with Nauru ($77.3), Tunisia ($77.2), Côte d'Ivoire ($80.2). The Honduras manufacturing per capita was less than manufacturing per capita in the world ($383.2) in 4.9 times, and was less than manufacturing per capita in the Americas ($896.7) in 11.4 times.

The growth of manufacturing in Honduras was 7.6% in the 1970s, ranked 39th in the world, and was on a par with DPRK (7.6%). The growth of manufacturing in Honduras (7.6%) was greater than growth of manufacturing in the world (3.8%), was greater than growth of manufacturing in the Americas (3.6%).

Comparison with neighbors. The manufacturing of Honduras was less than in Guatemala ($608.9 million), in Nicaragua ($362.2 million), and in El Salvador ($256.8 million). The manufacturing per capita in Honduras was greater than in El Salvador ($62.6); but less than in Nicaragua ($130.5) and in Guatemala ($95.8). The growth of manufacturing in Honduras was greater than in Guatemala (6.3%), in El Salvador (2.4%), and in Nicaragua (0.90%).

Comparison with leaders. The value added of manufacturing in Honduras was less than in the United States ($378.0 billion), in the USSR ($248.8 billion), in Japan ($169.3 billion), in Germany ($138.0 billion), and in France ($64.5 billion). The sector of manufacturing per capita in Honduras was less than in Germany ($1 752.1), in the United States ($1 731.8), in Japan ($1 520.6), in France ($1 203.0), and in the USSR ($986.6). The growth of manufacturing in Honduras was greater than in the USSR (5.2%), in Japan (4.5%), in France (3.5%), in the USA (2.7%), and in Germany (2.1%).

The 1980s

The manufacturing of Honduras was $687.1 million per year in the 1980s, ranked 87th in the world, and was on a par with Vietnam

($672.8 million), Afghanistan ($672.7 million). The share in the world was 0.021%, and 0.065% in the Americas.

The share of manufacturing in the economy of Honduras was 16.2% in the 1980s, ranked 81st in the world, and was on a par with Chile (16.2%), Greece (16.3%).

The manufacturing per capita in Honduras was $162.5 in the 1980s, ranked 99th in the world. The value of manufacturing per capita in Honduras was less than manufacturing per capita in the world ($661.2) in 4.1 times, and was less than manufacturing per capita in the Americas ($1 597.5) in 9.8 times.

The growth of manufacturing in Honduras was 2.4% in the 1980s, ranked 111th in the world. The growth of manufacturing in Honduras (2.4%) was less than growth of manufacturing in the world (2.6%), was greater than growth of manufacturing in the Americas (1.8%).

Comparison with neighbors. The manufacturing of Honduras was greater than in Nicaragua ($648.8 million) and in El Salvador ($585.1 million); but less than in Guatemala ($1.4 billion). The manufacturing per capita in Honduras was greater than in El Salvador ($119.4); but less than in Nicaragua ($176.2) and in Guatemala ($168.6). The growth of manufacturing in Honduras was greater than in El Salvador (0.28%), in Guatemala (0.19%), and in Nicaragua (-1.3%).

Comparison with leaders. The sector of manufacturing in Honduras was less than in the United States ($789.4 billion), in Japan ($501.0 billion), in the USSR ($305.7 billion), in Germany ($258.7 billion), and in Italy ($134.1 billion). The value of manufacturing per capita in Honduras was less than in Japan ($4.1 thousand), in Germany ($3.3 thousand), in the United States ($3.3 thousand), in Italy ($2.4 thousand), and in the USSR ($1 110.8). The growth of manufacturing in Honduras was greater than in the United States (1.9%) and in Germany (1.2%); but less than in the USSR (5.3%), in Japan (4.4%), and in Italy (2.5%).

The 1990s

The value added of manufacturing in Honduras was $890.5 million per year in the 1990s, ranked 95th in the world, and was on a par with Syria ($894.2 million). The share in the world was 0.017%, and 0.053% in the Americas.

The share of manufacturing in the economy of Honduras was 20.0% in the 1990s, ranked 54th in the world, and was on a par with Southern Africa (20.0%), Europe (19.9%), Côte d'Ivoire (19.9%).

The sector of manufacturing per capita in Honduras was $157.7 in the 1990s, ranked 125th in the world, and was on a par with Grenada ($157.9), Algeria ($158.1), Ivory Coast ($157.1). The value of manufacturing per capita in Honduras was less than manufacturing per capita in the world ($908.4) in 5.8 times, and was less than manufacturing per capita in the Americas ($2 172.9) in 13.8 times.

The growth of manufacturing in Honduras was 3.5% in the 1990s, ranked 76th in the world, and was on a par with Asia (3.5%). The growth of manufacturing in Honduras (3.5%) was greater than growth of manufacturing in the world (2.0%), was greater than growth of manufacturing in the Americas (3.0%).

Comparison with neighbors. The manufacturing of Honduras was greater than in Nicaragua ($554.2 million); but less than in Guatemala ($1.9 billion) and in El Salvador ($1.6 billion). The sector of manufacturing per capita in Honduras was greater than in Nicaragua ($120.6); but less than in El Salvador ($278.6) and in Guatemala ($188.7). The growth of manufacturing in Honduras was greater than in Nicaragua (2.8%) and in Guatemala (2.8%); but less than in El Salvador (7.0%).

Comparison with leaders. The manufacturing of Honduras was less than in the United States ($1.2 trillion), in Japan ($1.0 trillion), in Germany ($468.8 billion), in Italy ($227.8 billion), and in France ($215.0 billion). The manufacturing per capita in Honduras was less than in Japan ($8.3 thousand), in Germany ($5.8 thousand), in the United States ($4.7 thousand), in Italy ($4.0 thousand), and in France ($3.6 thousand). The growth of manufacturing in Honduras was greater than in the USA (3.2%), in France (2.4%), in Italy (1.2%), in Japan (1.1%), and in Germany (0.26%).

The 2000s

The Honduras manufacturing was $1.9 billion per year in the 2000s, ranked 97th in the world. The share in the world was 0.026%, and 0.083% in the Americas.

The share of manufacturing in the economy of Honduras was 19.5% in the 2000s, ranked 36th in the world, and was on a par with DPRK (19.5%), the Dominican Republic (19.5%), Switzerland (19.6%).

The value of manufacturing per capita in Honduras was $256.8 in the 2000s, ranked 123rd in the world, and was on a par with

Dominica ($253.7), Central Asia ($262.8). The value of manufacturing per capita in Honduras was less than manufacturing per capita in the world ($1 138.1) in 4.4 times, and was less than manufacturing per capita in the Americas ($2 583.7) in 10.1 times.

The growth of manufacturing in Honduras was 3.8% in the 2000s, ranked 81st in the world. The growth of manufacturing in Honduras (3.8%) was less than growth of manufacturing in the world (4.2%), was greater than growth of manufacturing in the Americas (1.4%).

Comparison with neighbors. The value added of manufacturing in Honduras was greater than in Nicaragua ($876.0 million); but less than in Guatemala ($3.8 billion) and in El Salvador ($2.6 billion). The value added of manufacturing per capita in Honduras was greater than in Nicaragua ($162.1); but less than in El Salvador ($423.8) and in Guatemala ($291.4). The growth of manufacturing in Honduras was greater than in Nicaragua (3.5%), in Guatemala (2.2%), and in El Salvador (0.14%).

Comparison with leaders. The value of manufacturing in Honduras was less than in the United States ($1.6 trillion), in China ($1.1 trillion), in Japan ($992.9 billion), in Germany ($551.4 billion), and in Italy ($277.2 billion). The value added of manufacturing per capita in Honduras was less than in Japan ($7.7 thousand), in Germany ($6.8 thousand), in the USA ($5.6 thousand), in Italy ($4.8 thousand), and in China ($815.3). The growth of manufacturing in Honduras was greater than in the United States (1.6%), in Japan (0.32%), in Germany (0.097%), and in Italy (-1.3%).

The 2010s

The value of manufacturing in Honduras was $3.5 billion per year in the 2010s, ranked 95th in the world, and was on a par with Estonia ($3.5 billion). The share in the world was 0.028%, and 0.12% in the Americas.

The share of manufacturing in the economy of Honduras was 17.6% in the 2010s, ranked 43rd in the world, and was on a par with El Salvador (17.7%), Central Asia (17.5%), Morocco (17.4%).

The sector of manufacturing per capita in Honduras was $388.1 in the 2010s, ranked 119th in the world, and was on a par with the Cook Islands ($388.5), Armenia ($393.7), Jamaica ($397.1). The Honduran manufacturing per capita was less than manufacturing per capita in the world ($1 697.4) in 4.4 times, and was less than manufacturing per capita in the Americas ($3 100.6) in 8.0 times.

The growth of manufacturing in Honduras was 3.4% in the 2010s, ranked 97th in the world, and was on a par with Oman (3.4%), Kenya (3.4%), Bahrain (3.4%). The growth of manufacturing in Honduras (3.4%) was less than growth of manufacturing in the world (3.9%), was greater than growth of manufacturing in the Americas (1.6%).

Comparison with neighbors. The sector of manufacturing in Honduras was 2.1 times higher than in Nicaragua ($1.7 billion); but 2.4 times lower than in Guatemala ($8.4 billion) and 5.5% lower than in El Salvador ($3.7 billion). The Honduran manufacturing per capita was 44.2% higher than in Nicaragua ($269.1); but 34.0% lower than in El Salvador ($587.6) and 26.1% lower than in Guatemala ($524.9). The growth of manufacturing in Honduras was greater than in Guatemala (3.2%) and in El Salvador (1.8%); but less than in Nicaragua (5.2%).

Comparison with leaders. The value added of manufacturing in Honduras was 888.5 times lower than in China ($3.1 trillion), 590.6 times lower than in the United States ($2.1 trillion), 302.3 times lower than in Japan ($1.1 trillion), 209.7 times lower than in Germany ($735.2 billion), and 111.4 times lower than in Republic of Korea ($390.5 billion). The Honduras manufacturing per capita was 23.1 times lower than in Germany ($9.0 thousand), 21.4 times lower than in Japan ($8.3 thousand), 19.9 times lower than in South Korea ($7.7 thousand), 16.7 times lower than in the USA ($6.5 thousand), and 5.7 times lower than in China ($2.2 thousand). The growth of manufacturing in Honduras was greater than in Japan (3.0%) and in the United States (1.9%); but less than in China (7.5%), in South Korea (3.8%), and in Germany (3.5%).

Chapter VI. Construction

(ISIC F)

The sector of construction in Honduras increased from $85.6 million per year in the 1970s to $1.2 billion per year in the 2010s, that is by $1.1 billion or 14.0 times. The change occurred at $1.0 billion due to a 7.8-fold increase in prices, as also at -$93.7 million due to a 1.6-fold decrease in productivity, as well as at $162.3 million due to the growth in population. The average annual growth in construction is 1.9%. The minimum value of construction was in 1972 at $46.6 million. The maximum value of construction was in 2019 at $1.6 billion.

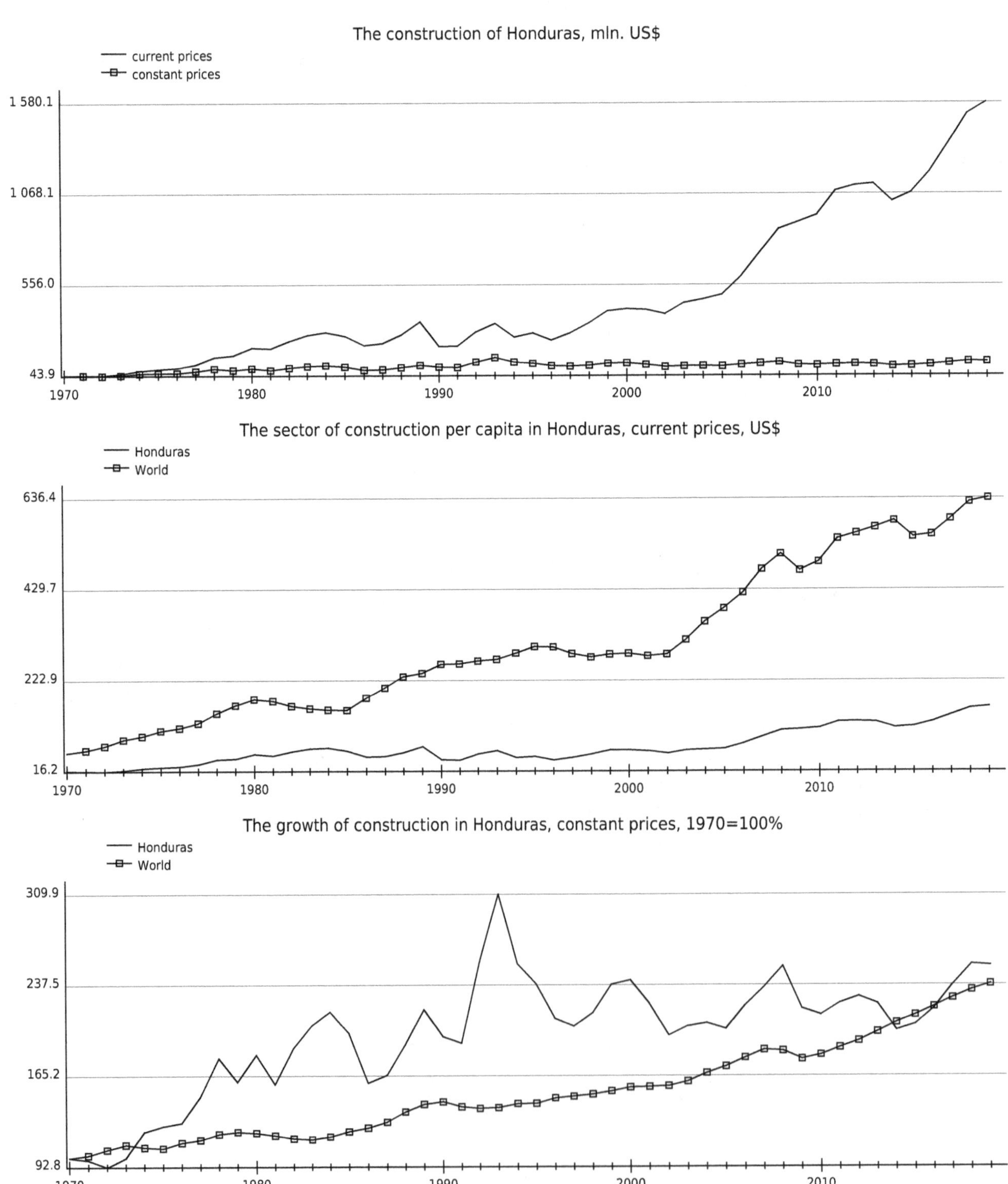

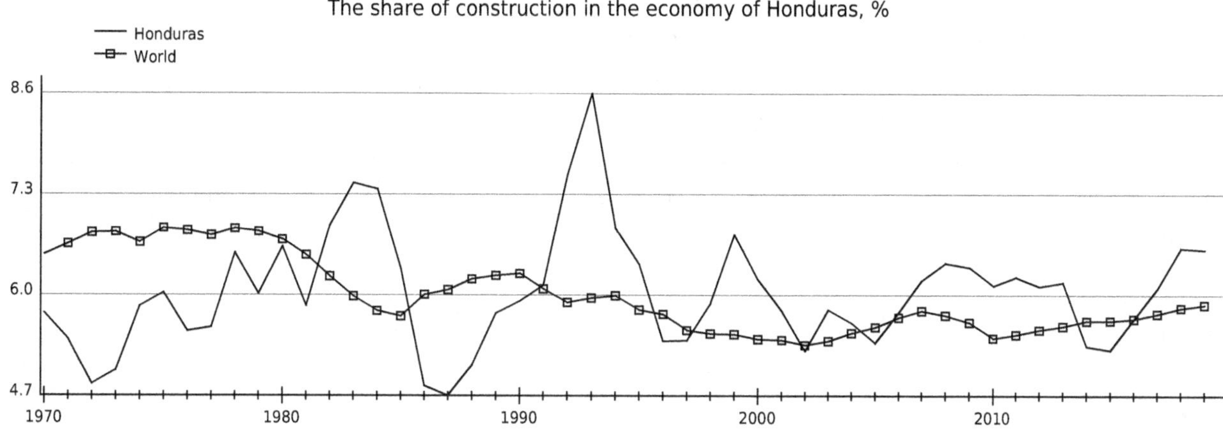

The 1970s

The sector of construction in Honduras was $85.6 million per year in the 1970s, ranked 101st in the world, and was on a par with Jordan ($87.2 million). The share in the world was 0.020%, and 0.070% in the Americas.

The share of construction in the economy of Honduras was 5.8% in the 1970s, ranked 103rd in the world, and was on a par with Jamaica (5.8%).

The value of construction per capita in Honduras was $27.4 in the 1970s, ranked 126th in the world, and was on a par with Zimbabwe ($26.9). The value added of construction per capita in Honduras was less than construction per capita in the world ($106.1) in 3.9 times, and was less than construction per capita in the Americas ($217.5) in 7.9 times.

The growth of construction in Honduras was 5.4% in the 1970s, ranked 83rd in the world, and was on a par with Cuba (5.4%). The growth of construction in Honduras (5.4%) was greater than growth of construction in the world (2.1%), was greater than growth of construction in the Americas (1.5%).

Comparison with neighbors. The value of construction in Honduras was greater than in El Salvador ($62.4 million); but less than in Nicaragua ($118.5 million) and in Guatemala ($91.0 million). The sector of construction per capita in Honduras was greater than in El Salvador ($15.2) and in Guatemala ($14.3); but less than in Nicaragua ($42.7). The growth of construction in Honduras was greater than in Nicaragua (-11.7%); but less than in Guatemala (14.3%) and in El Salvador (8.6%).

Comparison with leaders. The value of construction in Honduras was less than in the USA ($81.1 billion), in the USSR ($52.5 billion), in Japan ($43.5 billion), in Germany ($33.8 billion), and in France ($22.4 billion). The value of construction per capita in Honduras was less than in Germany ($428.6), in France ($417.3), in Japan ($390.8), in the USA ($371.5), and in the USSR ($208.1). The growth of construction in Honduras was greater than in Japan (3.4%), in France (2.0%), in Germany (0.66%), and in the USA (0.31%); but less than in the USSR (6.5%).

The 1980s

The value of construction in Honduras was $253.4 million per year in the 1980s, ranked 87th in the world, and was on a par with Albania ($255.2 million), Guinea ($251.1 million). The share in the world was 0.028%, and 0.096% in the Americas.

The share of construction in the economy of Honduras was 6.0% in the 1980s, ranked 82nd in the world, and was on a par with Portugal (6.0%), the Caribbean (5.9%).

The construction per capita in Honduras was $59.9 in the 1980s, ranked 115th in the world, and was on a par with the Philippines ($58.6). The sector of construction per capita in Honduras was less than construction per capita in the world ($186.2) in 3.1 times, and was less than construction per capita in the Americas ($396.8) in 6.6 times.

The growth of construction in Honduras was 3.1% in the 1980s, ranked 74th in the world, and was on a par with Palau (3.1%), Iceland (3.1%). The growth of construction in Honduras (3.1%) was greater than growth of construction in the world (1.7%), was greater than growth of construction in the Americas (0.83%).

Comparison with neighbors. The sector of construction in Honduras was greater than in Guatemala ($229.8 million), in Nicaragua ($162.1 million), and in El Salvador ($115.5 million). The sector of construction per capita in Honduras was greater than in Nicaragua

($44.0), in Guatemala ($28.2), and in El Salvador ($23.6). The growth of construction in Honduras was greater than in Guatemala (-2.5%) and in El Salvador (-3.7%); but less than in Nicaragua (9.4%).

Comparison with leaders. The construction of Honduras was less than in the United States ($180.6 billion), in Japan ($138.7 billion), in the USSR ($72.1 billion), in Germany ($57.8 billion), and in France ($42.5 billion). The value of construction per capita in Honduras was less than in Japan ($1 143.9), in the USA ($754.4), in France ($751.9), in Germany ($740.2), and in the USSR ($262.0). The growth of construction in Honduras was greater than in Japan (2.1%), in the USA (1.1%), in France (0.67%), and in Germany (-0.52%); but less than in the USSR (6.2%).

The 1990s

The value of construction in Honduras was $287.2 million per year in the 1990s, ranked 103rd in the world, and was on a par with Palestine ($286.7 million), Panama ($283.6 million), Botswana ($291.7 million). The share in the world was 0.018%, and 0.066% in the Americas.

The share of construction in the economy of Honduras was 6.4% in the 1990s, ranked 67th in the world, and was on a par with Micronesia (6.4%), Guyana (6.5%), Portugal (6.5%).

The sector of construction per capita in Honduras was $50.9 in the 1990s, ranked 140th in the world, and was on a par with Bhutan ($49.9), Morocco ($49.7), Azerbaijan ($49.7). The construction per capita in Honduras was less than construction per capita in the world ($278.6) in 5.5 times, and was less than construction per capita in the Americas ($564.1) in 11.1 times.

The growth of construction in Honduras was 0.9% in the 1990s, ranked 131st in the world. The growth of construction in Honduras (0.87%) was greater than growth of construction in the world (0.71%), was less than growth of construction in the Americas (1.8%).

Comparison with neighbors. The sector of construction in Honduras was greater than in Nicaragua ($178.9 million); but less than in Guatemala ($453.0 million) and in El Salvador ($342.9 million). The value of construction per capita in Honduras was greater than in Guatemala ($44.0) and in Nicaragua ($38.9); but less than in El Salvador ($61.5). The growth of construction in Honduras was less than in El Salvador (9.8%), in Guatemala (5.1%), and in Nicaragua (4.0%).

Comparison with leaders. The value added of construction in Honduras was less than in Japan ($343.2 billion), in the United States ($299.1 billion), in Germany ($125.2 billion), in the UK ($69.8 billion), and in France ($68.8 billion). The value of construction per capita in Honduras was less than in Japan ($2.7 thousand), in Germany ($1 552.3), in the United Kingdom ($1 205.1), in France ($1 158.8), and in the USA ($1 131.2). The growth of construction in Honduras was greater than in Germany (-0.047%), in the United Kingdom (-0.34%), in France (-0.65%), and in Japan (-1.0%); but less than in the United States (1.8%).

The 2000s

The Honduras construction was $577.1 million per year in the 2000s, ranked 112th in the world, and was on a par with Uganda ($585.7 million), Equatorial Guinea ($587.5 million). The share in the world was 0.023%, and 0.071% in the Americas.

The share of construction in the economy of Honduras was 5.9% in the 2000s, ranked 93rd in the world, and was on a par with San Marino (5.9%), Western Asia (6.0%), the Seychelles (6.0%).

The Honduras construction per capita was $78.3 in the 2000s, ranked 140th in the world, and was on a par with Fiji ($78.8). The construction per capita in Honduras was less than construction per capita in the world ($381.3) in 4.9 times, and was less than construction per capita in the Americas ($931.0) in 11.9 times.

The growth of construction in Honduras was -0.8% in the 2000s, ranked 193rd in the world, and was on a par with Aruba (-0.82%). The growth of construction in Honduras (-0.83%) was less than growth of construction in the world (1.5%), was greater than growth of construction in the Americas (-0.96%).

Comparison with neighbors. The construction of Honduras was greater than in Nicaragua ($313.8 million); but less than in Guatemala ($1.3 billion) and in El Salvador ($712.4 million). The Honduran construction per capita was greater than in Nicaragua ($58.1); but less than in El Salvador ($118.1) and in Guatemala ($102.9). The growth of construction in Honduras was greater than in Nicaragua (-5.4%); but less than in El Salvador (2.8%) and in Guatemala (0.58%).

Comparison with leaders. The Honduras construction was less than in the United States ($583.0 billion), in Japan ($270.5 billion), in China ($150.1 billion), in the UK ($132.1 billion), and in Spain ($111.8 billion). The Honduras construction per capita was less than in

Spain ($2.6 thousand), in the UK ($2.2 thousand), in Japan ($2.1 thousand), in the USA ($1 983.7), and in China ($113.1). The growth of construction in Honduras was greater than in the USA (-2.6%) and in Japan (-3.9%); but less than in China (11.9%), in Spain (1.7%), and in the UK (0.17%).

The 2010s

The value of construction in Honduras was $1.2 billion per year in the 2010s, ranked 111th in the world, and was on a par with Yemen ($1.2 billion), Libya ($1.2 billion), Cyprus ($1.2 billion). The share in the world was 0.029%, and 0.10% in the Americas.

The share of construction in the economy of Honduras was 6.0% in the 2010s, ranked 103rd in the world, and was on a par with Curaçao (6.0%), São Tomé and Príncipe (6.0%), South Sudan (6.0%).

The value added of construction per capita in Honduras was $132.9 in the 2010s, ranked 152nd in the world, and was on a par with Vanuatu ($134.9). The construction per capita in Honduras was less than construction per capita in the world ($572.1) in 4.3 times, and was less than construction per capita in the Americas ($1 189.0) in 8.9 times.

The growth of construction in Honduras was 1.4% in the 2010s, ranked 136th in the world. The growth of construction in Honduras (1.4%) was less than growth of construction in the world (2.9%), was greater than growth of construction in the Americas (1.3%).

Comparison with neighbors. The Honduran construction was 2.1 times higher than in Nicaragua ($568.4 million); but 2.3 times lower than in Guatemala ($2.8 billion) and 2.0% lower than in El Salvador ($1.2 billion). The Honduras construction per capita was 44.6% higher than in Nicaragua ($91.9); but 31.5% lower than in El Salvador ($193.9) and 23.9% lower than in Guatemala ($174.5). The growth of construction in Honduras was greater than in Nicaragua (-0.78%); but less than in El Salvador (4.1%) and in Guatemala (1.7%).

Comparison with leaders. The value added of construction in Honduras was 609.0 times lower than in China ($731.1 billion), 567.1 times lower than in the United States ($680.8 billion), 232.1 times lower than in Japan ($278.7 billion), 140.0 times lower than in India ($168.1 billion), and 127.6 times lower than in Germany ($153.2 billion). The construction per capita in Honduras was 2.9% higher than in India ($129.1); but 16.4 times lower than in Japan ($2.2 thousand), 16.0 times lower than in the United States ($2.1 thousand), 14.1 times lower than in Germany ($1 871.9), and 3.9 times lower than in China ($521.3). The growth of construction in Honduras was greater than in the USA (1.4%); but less than in China (8.2%), in India (5.2%), in Germany (1.8%), and in Japan (1.7%).

Chapter VII. Transportation

Transport, storage and communication (ISIC I)

The transportation of Honduras grew up from $141.3 million per year in the 1970s to $1.4 billion per year in the 2010s, that is by $1.3 billion or 9.9 times. The change occurred at $101.2 million due to a 1.1-fold increase in prices, as also at $884.0 million due to a 3.2-fold increase in productivity, as well as at $267.9 million due to the increase in population. The average annual growth in transportation is 5.3%. The minimum value of transportation was in 1970 at $73.9 million. The maximum value of transportation was in 2019 at $1.8 billion.

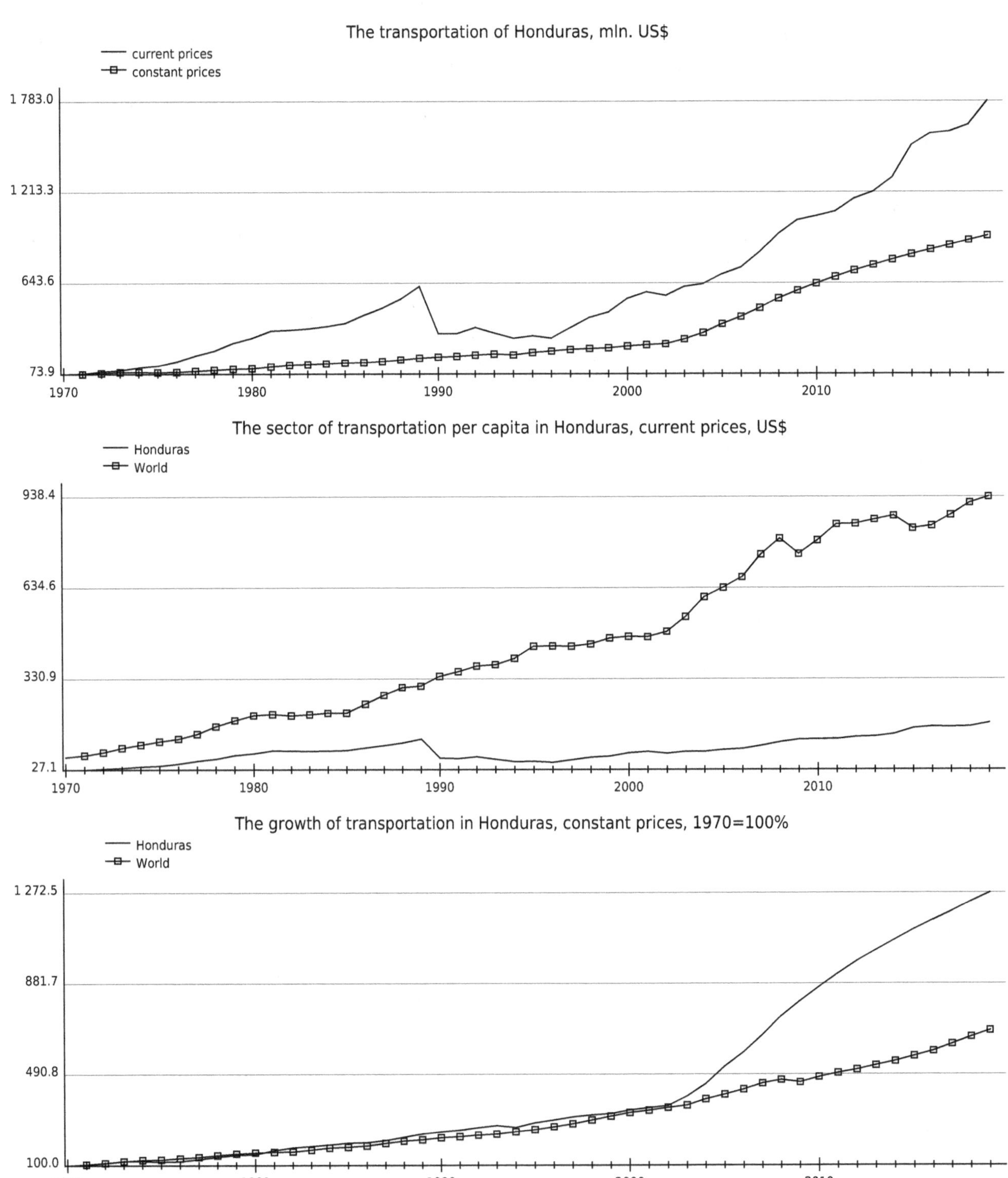

The transportation of Honduras, mln. US$

The sector of transportation per capita in Honduras, current prices, US$

The growth of transportation in Honduras, constant prices, 1970=100%

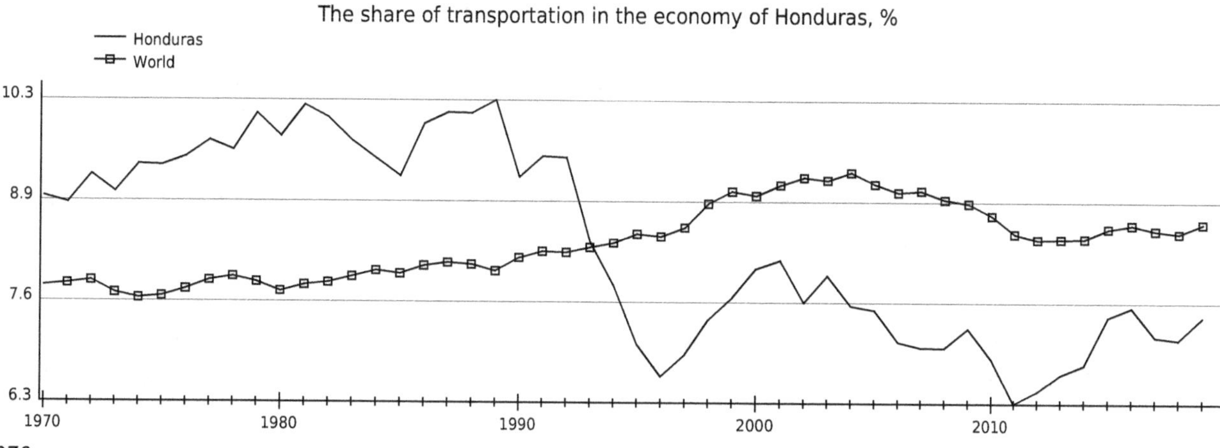

The 1970s

The value of transportation in Honduras was $141.3 million per year in the 1970s, ranked 93rd in the world, and was on a par with Bolivia ($141.9 million). The share in the world was 0.029%, and 0.070% in the Americas.

The share of transportation in the economy of Honduras was 9.5% in the 1970s, ranked 39th in the world, and was on a par with the UK (9.5%), Melanesia (9.5%), Greece (9.5%).

The transportation per capita in Honduras was $45.3 in the 1970s, ranked 108th in the world, and was on a par with the Federated States of Micronesia ($45.3), Grenada ($46.0), Oman ($44.2). The Honduras transportation per capita was less than transportation per capita in the world ($122.3) in 2.7 times, and was less than transportation per capita in the Americas ($360.9) in 8.0 times.

The growth of transportation in Honduras was 4.1% in the 1970s, ranked 121st in the world, and was on a par with Bhutan (4.1%), France (4.1%). The growth of transportation in Honduras (4.1%) was less than growth of transportation in the world (4.6%), was less than growth of transportation in the Americas (4.9%).

Comparison with neighbors. The sector of transportation in Honduras was greater than in El Salvador ($67.8 million); but less than in Nicaragua ($228.4 million) and in Guatemala ($155.4 million). The value added of transportation per capita in Honduras was greater than in Guatemala ($24.4) and in El Salvador ($16.5); but less than in Nicaragua ($82.3). The growth of transportation in Honduras was greater than in El Salvador (0.28%) and in Nicaragua (-0.90%); but less than in Guatemala (8.2%).

Comparison with leaders. The value of transportation in Honduras was less than in the USA ($168.6 billion), in Japan ($46.4 billion), in Germany ($29.6 billion), in the USSR ($28.8 billion), and in France ($24.0 billion). The sector of transportation per capita in Honduras was less than in the United States ($772.4), in France ($447.4), in Japan ($416.6), in Germany ($376.1), and in the USSR ($114.0). The growth of transportation in Honduras was greater than in Germany (3.0%) and in Japan (1.7%); but less than in the USSR (8.1%), in the USA (4.2%), and in France (4.1%).

The 1980s

The value of transportation in Honduras was $421.4 million per year in the 1980s, ranked 82nd in the world, and was on a par with Cyprus ($425.8 million). The share in the world was 0.036%, and 0.089% in the Americas.

The share of transportation in the economy of Honduras was 9.9% in the 1980s, ranked 36th in the world, and was on a par with Mongolia (9.9%), Finland (9.9%), Kiribati (9.9%).

The Honduras transportation per capita was $99.6 in the 1980s, ranked 102nd in the world, and was on a par with Argentina ($99.6), Vanuatu ($97.7), South America ($101.7). The transportation per capita in Honduras was less than transportation per capita in the world ($242.0) in 2.4 times, and was less than transportation per capita in the Americas ($714.8) in 7.2 times.

The growth of transportation in Honduras was 5% in the 1980s, ranked 50th in the world, and was on a par with Syria (5.0%), Mauritius (5.0%), Benin (5.1%). The growth of transportation in Honduras (5.0%) was greater than growth of transportation in the world (3.4%), was greater than growth of transportation in the Americas (3.5%).

Comparison with neighbors. The value added of transportation in Honduras was greater than in Guatemala ($359.0 million), in Nicaragua ($324.3 million), and in El Salvador ($165.9 million). The sector of transportation per capita in Honduras was greater than in

Nicaragua ($88.1), in Guatemala ($44.0), and in El Salvador ($33.9). The growth of transportation in Honduras was greater than in Guatemala (2.5%), in El Salvador (1.3%), and in Nicaragua (-1.5%).

Comparison with leaders. The value added of transportation in Honduras was less than in the United States ($394.9 billion), in Japan ($147.7 billion), in Germany ($56.6 billion), in France ($56.2 billion), and in the United Kingdom ($53.0 billion). The sector of transportation per capita in Honduras was less than in the USA ($1 649.2), in Japan ($1 217.8), in France ($993.7), in the UK ($938.7), and in Germany ($725.5). The growth of transportation in Honduras was greater than in Japan (4.7%), in the United States (3.6%), in the United Kingdom (3.0%), and in Germany (1.8%); but less than in France (5.4%).

The 1990s

The Honduran transportation was $351.7 million per year in the 1990s, ranked 113th in the world, and was on a par with Madagascar ($353.0 million), French Polynesia ($353.8 million), Malta ($360.0 million). The share in the world was 0.015%, and 0.041% in the Americas.

The share of transportation in the economy of Honduras was 7.9% in the 1990s, ranked 101st in the world, and was on a par with Central Asia (7.9%), Tuvalu (7.9%), Middle Africa (7.9%).

The value of transportation per capita in Honduras was $62.3 in the 1990s, ranked 143rd in the world, and was on a par with Africa ($63.1), Kosovo ($63.3), Nicaragua ($61.2). The value added of transportation per capita in Honduras was less than transportation per capita in the world ($409.5) in 6.6 times, and was less than transportation per capita in the Americas ($1 104.4) in 17.7 times.

The growth of transportation in Honduras was 3.2% in the 1990s, ranked 131st in the world, and was on a par with Southern Europe (3.2%), Poland (3.2%), South America (3.2%). The growth of transportation in Honduras (3.2%) was less than growth of transportation in the world (4.0%), was less than growth of transportation in the Americas (4.7%).

Comparison with neighbors. The value of transportation in Honduras was greater than in Nicaragua ($281.0 million); but less than in El Salvador ($595.6 million) and in Guatemala ($590.7 million). The value of transportation per capita in Honduras was greater than in Nicaragua ($61.2) and in Guatemala ($57.3); but less than in El Salvador ($106.8). The growth of transportation in Honduras was less than in El Salvador (11.5%), in Guatemala (6.0%), and in Nicaragua (3.6%).

Comparison with leaders. The value added of transportation in Honduras was less than in the USA ($702.6 billion), in Japan ($373.9 billion), in Germany ($144.3 billion), in France ($118.7 billion), and in the United Kingdom ($117.6 billion). The sector of transportation per capita in Honduras was less than in Japan ($3.0 thousand), in the USA ($2.7 thousand), in the UK ($2.0 thousand), in France ($1 999.2), and in Germany ($1 789.0). The growth of transportation in Honduras was greater than in Japan (3.0%); but less than in the USA (5.0%), in France (4.8%), in the UK (4.7%), and in Germany (3.9%).

The 2000s

The Honduran transportation was $722.0 million per year in the 2000s, ranked 113th in the world, and was on a par with Nepal ($730.6 million). The share in the world was 0.018%, and 0.049% in the Americas.

The share of transportation in the economy of Honduras was 7.4% in the 2000s, ranked 146th in the world, and was on a par with Suriname (7.4%), Western Africa (7.4%), Aruba (7.4%).

The transportation per capita in Honduras was $98.0 in the 2000s, ranked 153rd in the world, and was on a par with Africa ($99.3), Nigeria ($95.8), the Philippines ($95.8). The sector of transportation per capita in Honduras was less than transportation per capita in the world ($621.1) in 6.3 times, and was less than transportation per capita in the Americas ($1 687.7) in 17.2 times.

The growth of transportation in Honduras was 9.6% in the 2000s, ranked 37th in the world, and was on a par with Serbia (9.6%). The growth of transportation in Honduras (9.6%) was greater than growth of transportation in the world (3.9%), was greater than growth of transportation in the Americas (3.2%).

Comparison with neighbors. The value of transportation in Honduras was greater than in Nicaragua ($376.9 million); but less than in Guatemala ($1.7 billion) and in El Salvador ($1.3 billion). The value of transportation per capita in Honduras was greater than in Nicaragua ($69.8); but less than in El Salvador ($213.7) and in Guatemala ($127.6). The growth of transportation in Honduras was greater than in Nicaragua (5.7%) and in El Salvador (2.6%); but less than in Guatemala (11.6%).

Comparison with leaders. The transportation of Honduras was less than in the United States ($1.2 trillion), in Japan ($468.5 billion), in

Germany ($228.2 billion), in the United Kingdom ($215.9 billion), and in France ($185.6 billion). The sector of transportation per capita in Honduras was less than in the United States ($4.0 thousand), in Japan ($3.7 thousand), in the UK ($3.6 thousand), in France ($3.0 thousand), and in Germany ($2.8 thousand). The growth of transportation in Honduras was greater than in Germany (3.4%), in the UK (3.1%), in the United States (3.1%), in France (2.7%), and in Japan (1.5%).

The 2010s

The transportation of Honduras was $1.4 billion per year in the 2010s, ranked 116th in the world, and was on a par with Georgia ($1.4 billion), Trinidad and Tobago ($1.4 billion). The share in the world was 0.022%, and 0.060% in the Americas.

The share of transportation in the economy of Honduras was 7.0% in the 2010s, ranked 153rd in the world, and was on a par with Bahrain (7.0%), Gambia (7.0%), Armenia (7.0%).

The value of transportation per capita in Honduras was $154.3 in the 2010s, ranked 161st in the world, and was on a par with Syria ($154.6). The transportation per capita in Honduras was less than transportation per capita in the world ($864.8) in 5.6 times, and was less than transportation per capita in the Americas ($2 381.9) in 15.4 times.

The growth of transportation in Honduras was 4.7% in the 2010s, ranked 93rd in the world, and was on a par with the Americas (4.7%), San Marino (4.7%). The growth of transportation in Honduras (4.7%) was greater than growth of transportation in the world (4.0%), was less than growth of transportation in the Americas (4.7%).

Comparison with neighbors. The value of transportation in Honduras was 2.3 times higher than in Nicaragua ($597.7 million); but 3.1 times lower than in Guatemala ($4.3 billion) and 24.3% lower than in El Salvador ($1.8 billion). The transportation per capita in Honduras was 59.7% higher than in Nicaragua ($96.7); but 47.1% lower than in El Salvador ($291.7) and 42.4% lower than in Guatemala ($268.0). The growth of transportation in Honduras was greater than in Guatemala (3.7%) and in El Salvador (1.3%); but less than in Nicaragua (5.2%).

Comparison with leaders. The sector of transportation in Honduras was 1 282.6 times lower than in the USA ($1.8 trillion), 380.0 times lower than in Japan ($529.8 billion), 332.9 times lower than in China ($464.2 billion), 215.2 times lower than in Germany ($300.0 billion), and 184.8 times lower than in the UK ($257.7 billion). The sector of transportation per capita in Honduras was 36.3 times lower than in the United States ($5.6 thousand), 26.8 times lower than in Japan ($4.1 thousand), 25.5 times lower than in the United Kingdom ($3.9 thousand), 23.7 times lower than in Germany ($3.7 thousand), and 2.1 times lower than in China ($331.0). The growth of transportation in Honduras was greater than in the UK (2.8%), in Germany (2.7%), and in Japan (0.81%); but less than in China (7.5%) and in the United States (5.1%).

Chapter VIII. Trade

Wholesale, retail trade, restaurants and hotels (ISIC G-H)

The sector of trade in Honduras grew up from $262.4 million per year in the 1970s to $3.5 billion per year in the 2010s, that is by $3.2 billion or 13.2 times. The change occurred at $2.8 billion due to a 5.2-fold increase in prices, as also at -$94.0 million due to a 1.1-fold decrease in productivity, as well as at $497.4 million due to the growing in population. The average annual growth in trade is 2.7%. The minimum value of trade was in 1970 at $141.1 million. The maximum value of trade was in 2019 at $4.2 billion.

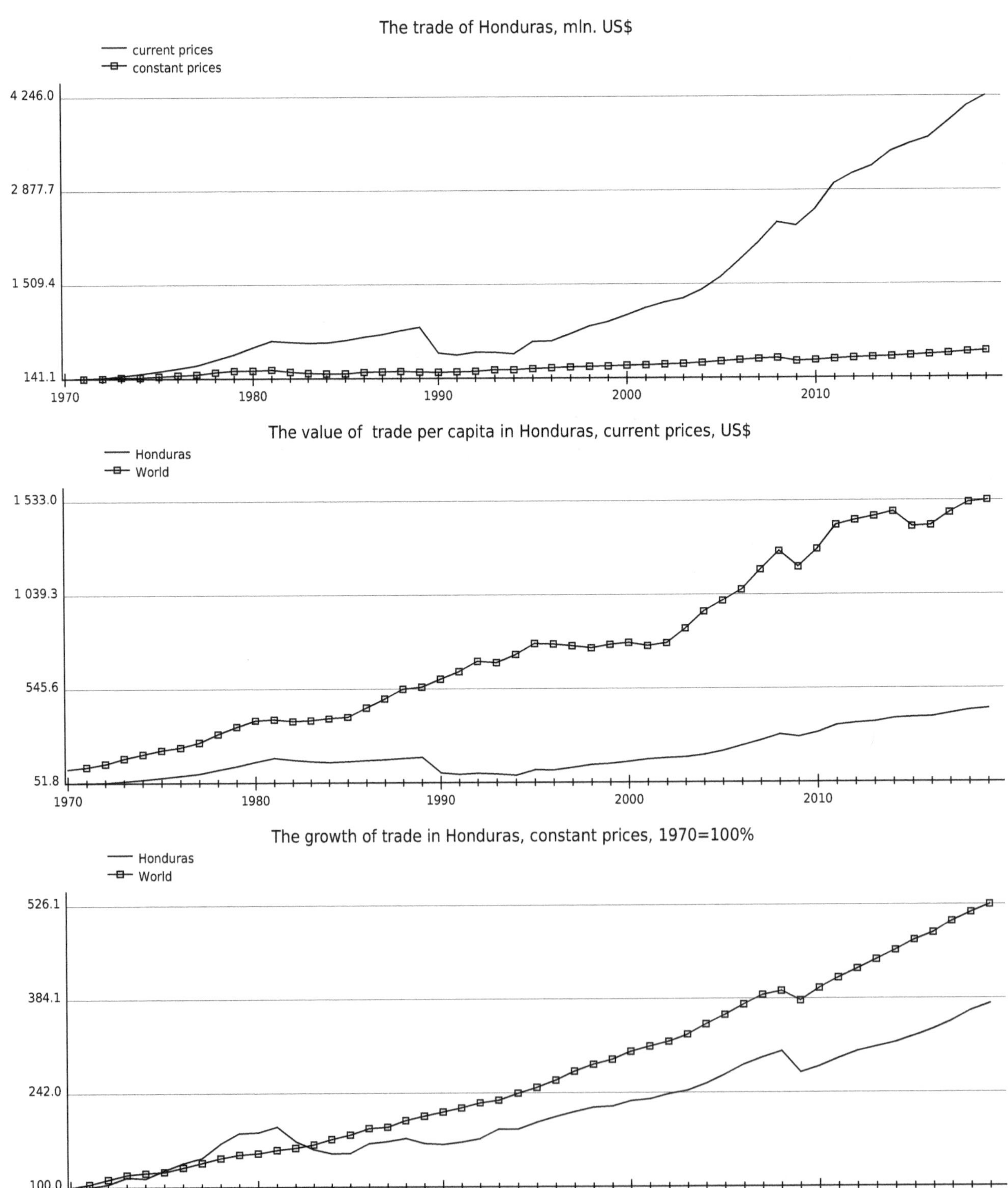

The trade of Honduras, mln. US$

The value of trade per capita in Honduras, current prices, US$

The growth of trade in Honduras, constant prices, 1970=100%

The 1970s

The Honduras trade was $262.4 million per year in the 1970s, ranked 98th in the world, and was on a par with Kenya ($264.7 million), Monaco ($259.1 million). The share in the world was 0.029%, and 0.072% in the Americas.

The share of trade in the economy of Honduras was 17.7% in the 1970s, ranked 55th in the world, and was on a par with Bermuda (17.6%), Argentina (17.6%), Sudan (17.8%).

The trade per capita in Honduras was $84.1 in the 1970s, ranked 118th in the world, and was on a par with the FSM ($84.1), Kiribati ($85.7), Thailand ($86.2). The value added of trade per capita in Honduras was less than trade per capita in the world ($221.0) in 2.6 times, and was less than trade per capita in the Americas ($654.8) in 7.8 times.

The growth of trade in Honduras was 6.9% in the 1970s, ranked 51st in the world. The growth of trade in Honduras (6.9%) was greater than growth of trade in the world (4.5%), was greater than growth of trade in the Americas (4.4%).

Comparison with neighbors. The trade of Honduras was less than in Guatemala ($488.1 million), in El Salvador ($427.5 million), and in Nicaragua ($340.8 million). The Honduran trade per capita was greater than in Guatemala ($76.8); but less than in Nicaragua ($122.8) and in El Salvador ($104.2). The growth of trade in Honduras was greater than in El Salvador (5.6%), in Guatemala (5.3%), and in Nicaragua (-2.8%).

Comparison with leaders. The Honduras trade was less than in the USA ($278.3 billion), in Japan ($90.3 billion), in the USSR ($62.3 billion), in Germany ($61.1 billion), and in France ($40.9 billion). The value of trade per capita in Honduras was less than in the USA ($1 275.1), in Japan ($811.1), in Germany ($775.5), in France ($762.4), and in the USSR ($247.1). The growth of trade in Honduras was greater than in the USSR (5.2%), in France (3.9%), in the United States (3.9%), and in Germany (3.0%); but less than in Japan (8.2%).

The 1980s

The value of trade in Honduras was $722.7 million per year in the 1980s, ranked 88th in the world. The share in the world was 0.034%, and 0.086% in the Americas.

The share of trade in the economy of Honduras was 17.0% in the 1980s, ranked 64th in the world, and was on a par with Nicaragua (17.1%), the UAE (17.0%).

The Honduras trade per capita was $170.9 in the 1980s, ranked 109th in the world, and was on a par with the Comoros ($174.5), Asia ($166.8). The Honduran trade per capita was less than trade per capita in the world ($437.7) in 2.6 times, and was less than trade per capita in the Americas ($1 268.0) in 7.4 times.

The growth of trade in Honduras was -0.9% in the 1980s, ranked 168th in the world. The growth of trade in Honduras (-0.92%) was less than growth of trade in the world (3.3%), was less than growth of trade in the Americas (3.5%).

Comparison with neighbors. The trade of Honduras was greater than in Nicaragua ($542.3 million); but less than in Guatemala ($1.1 billion) and in El Salvador ($1.1 billion). The trade per capita in Honduras was greater than in Nicaragua ($147.3) and in Guatemala ($138.4); but less than in El Salvador ($227.8). The growth of trade in Honduras was less than in El Salvador (1.9%), in Guatemala (-0.26%), and in Nicaragua (-0.76%).

Comparison with leaders. The sector of trade in Honduras was less than in the USA ($653.3 billion), in Japan ($277.3 billion), in Germany ($116.7 billion), in the USSR ($112.3 billion), and in Italy ($95.7 billion). The Honduras trade per capita was less than in the United States ($2.7 thousand), in Japan ($2.3 thousand), in Italy ($1 684.2), in Germany ($1 496.0), and in the USSR ($408.1). The growth of trade in Honduras was less than in Japan (4.9%), in the USA (4.4%), in Italy (2.3%), in Germany (1.8%), and in the USSR (-0.62%).

The 1990s

The sector of trade in Honduras was $652.8 million per year in the 1990s, ranked 115th in the world, and was on a par with Qatar ($639.6 million). The share in the world was 0.016%, and 0.044% in the Americas.

The share of trade in the economy of Honduras was 14.6% in the 1990s, ranked 100th in the world, and was on a par with Europe (14.7%), the Netherlands (14.6%), Sri Lanka (14.6%).

The trade per capita in Honduras was $115.6 in the 1990s, ranked 143rd in the world, and was on a par with Guyana ($113.8). The value added of trade per capita in Honduras was less than trade per capita in the world ($721.8) in 6.2 times, and was less than trade per capita in the Americas ($1 943.2) in 16.8 times.

The growth of trade in Honduras was 2.9% in the 1990s, ranked 104th in the world, and was on a par with Malawi (2.9%), Austria (2.9%). The growth of trade in Honduras (2.9%) was less than growth of trade in the world (3.5%), was less than growth of trade in the Americas (3.8%).

Comparison with neighbors. The trade of Honduras was less than in Guatemala ($1.9 billion), in El Salvador ($1.4 billion), and in Nicaragua ($711.4 million). The sector of trade per capita in Honduras was less than in El Salvador ($247.6), in Guatemala ($180.1), and in Nicaragua ($154.8). The growth of trade in Honduras was greater than in El Salvador (-2.8%); but less than in Guatemala (4.1%) and in Nicaragua (4.0%).

Comparison with leaders. The trade of Honduras was less than in the USA ($1.2 trillion), in Japan ($713.2 billion), in Germany ($243.7 billion), in Italy ($185.6 billion), and in France ($177.0 billion). The value of trade per capita in Honduras was less than in Japan ($5.7 thousand), in the United States ($4.4 thousand), in Italy ($3.3 thousand), in Germany ($3.0 thousand), and in France ($3.0 thousand). The growth of trade in Honduras was greater than in Germany (2.5%), in France (2.4%), and in Italy (1.9%); but less than in the United States (4.3%) and in Japan (3.8%).

The 2000s

The trade of Honduras was $1.7 billion per year in the 2000s, ranked 105th in the world, and was on a par with DR Congo ($1.6 billion), Uganda ($1.6 billion), Bosnia and Herzegovina ($1.6 billion). The share in the world was 0.026%, and 0.068% in the Americas.

The share of trade in the economy of Honduras was 17.0% in the 2000s, ranked 71st in the world, and was on a par with Latvia (17.0%), Argentina (17.1%), Nigeria (17.0%).

The sector of trade per capita in Honduras was $224.6 in the 2000s, ranked 139th in the world, and was on a par with Nigeria ($219.6). The value added of trade per capita in Honduras was less than trade per capita in the world ($990.3) in 4.4 times, and was less than trade per capita in the Americas ($2 770.2) in 12.3 times.

The growth of trade in Honduras was 2.1% in the 2000s, ranked 147th in the world, and was on a par with Luxembourg (2.1%). The growth of trade in Honduras (2.1%) was less than growth of trade in the world (2.7%), was greater than growth of trade in the Americas (1.6%).

Comparison with neighbors. The value of trade in Honduras was greater than in Nicaragua ($971.7 million); but less than in Guatemala ($4.6 billion) and in El Salvador ($2.1 billion). The trade per capita in Honduras was greater than in Nicaragua ($179.8); but less than in Guatemala ($355.1) and in El Salvador ($353.7). The growth of trade in Honduras was greater than in El Salvador (1.1%); but less than in Guatemala (2.7%) and in Nicaragua (2.6%).

Comparison with leaders. The value of trade in Honduras was less than in the USA ($1.9 trillion), in Japan ($771.8 billion), in Germany ($296.0 billion), in the UK ($293.5 billion), and in China ($262.0 billion). The sector of trade per capita in Honduras was greater than in China ($197.5); but less than in the United States ($6.4 thousand), in Japan ($6.0 thousand), in the United Kingdom ($4.9 thousand), and in Germany ($3.6 thousand). The growth of trade in Honduras was greater than in Germany (1.7%), in the United Kingdom (1.3%), in the United States (1.1%), and in Japan (-0.77%); but less than in China (11.9%).

The 2010s

The value of trade in Honduras was $3.5 billion per year in the 2010s, ranked 104th in the world, and was on a par with Jordan ($3.5 billion). The share in the world was 0.033%, and 0.094% in the Americas.

The share of trade in the economy of Honduras was 17.5% in the 2010s, ranked 74th in the world, and was on a par with Fiji (17.5%), Sudan (17.5%), Ethiopia (17.4%).

The Honduras trade per capita was $384.8 in the 2010s, ranked 148th in the world, and was on a par with Jordan ($394.6). The sector of trade per capita in Honduras was less than trade per capita in the world ($1 436.8) in 3.7 times, and was less than trade per capita in the Americas ($3 802.7) in 9.9 times.

The growth of trade in Honduras was 3.3% in the 2010s, ranked 112th in the world, and was on a par with the World (3.3%), Latvia (3.3%). The growth of trade in Honduras (3.3%) was less than growth of trade in the world (3.3%), was greater than growth of trade in the Americas (2.1%).

Comparison with neighbors. The value of trade in Honduras was 5.7% higher than in El Salvador ($3.3 billion) and 2.0 times higher than in Nicaragua ($1.7 billion); but 3.7 times lower than in Guatemala ($12.7 billion). The sector of trade per capita in Honduras was 38.4% higher than in Nicaragua ($278.1); but 2.1 times lower than in Guatemala ($791.9) and 26.1% lower than in El Salvador ($521.1). The growth of trade in Honduras was greater than in Nicaragua (2.5%) and in El Salvador (2.1%); but less than in Guatemala (3.5%).

Comparison with leaders. The Honduran trade was 752.3 times lower than in the USA ($2.6 trillion), 343.6 times lower than in China ($1.2 trillion), 250.1 times lower than in Japan ($869.5 billion), 107.2 times lower than in Germany ($372.6 billion), and 94.9 times lower than in the United Kingdom ($330.0 billion). The value of trade per capita in Honduras was 21.3 times lower than in the United States ($8.2 thousand), 17.7 times lower than in Japan ($6.8 thousand), 13.1 times lower than in the UK ($5.0 thousand), 11.8 times lower than in Germany ($4.6 thousand), and 2.2 times lower than in China ($851.7). The growth of trade in Honduras was greater than in the UK (2.8%), in the United States (2.3%), in Germany (2.0%), and in Japan (0.77%); but less than in China (8.9%).

Chapter IX. Services

(ISIC J-P)

The value of services in Honduras enlarged from $337.5 million per year in the 1970s to $7.2 billion per year in the 2010s, that is by $6.8 billion or 21.2 times. The change occurred at $4.7 billion due to a 3.0-fold increase in prices, as also at $1.4 billion due to a 2.5-fold increase in productivity, as well as at $639.7 million due to the increase in population. The average annual growth in services is 5.3%. The minimum value of services was in 1970 at $186.4 million. The maximum value of services was in 2019 at $8.4 billion.

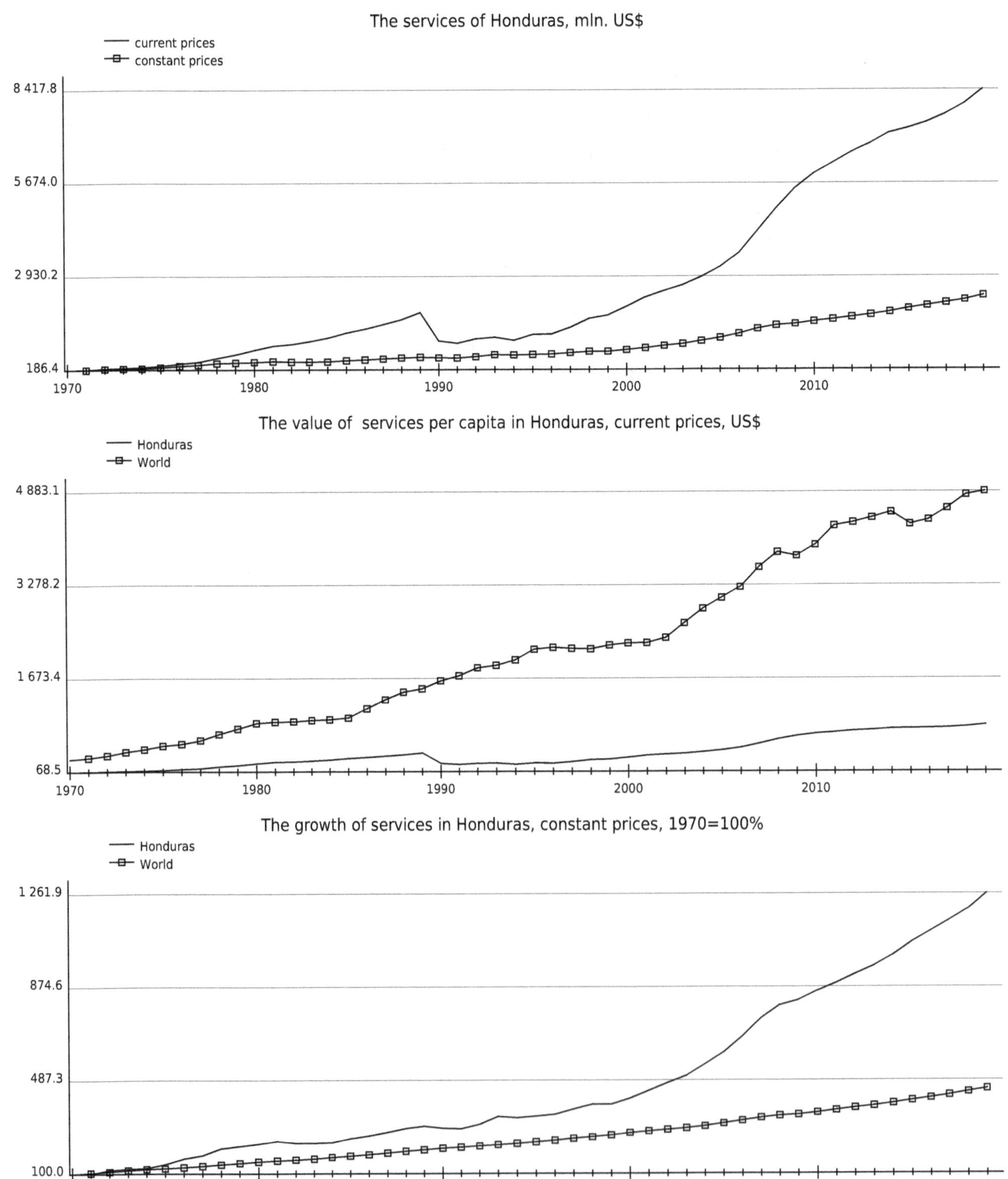

The services of Honduras, mln. US$

The value of services per capita in Honduras, current prices, US$

The growth of services in Honduras, constant prices, 1970=100%

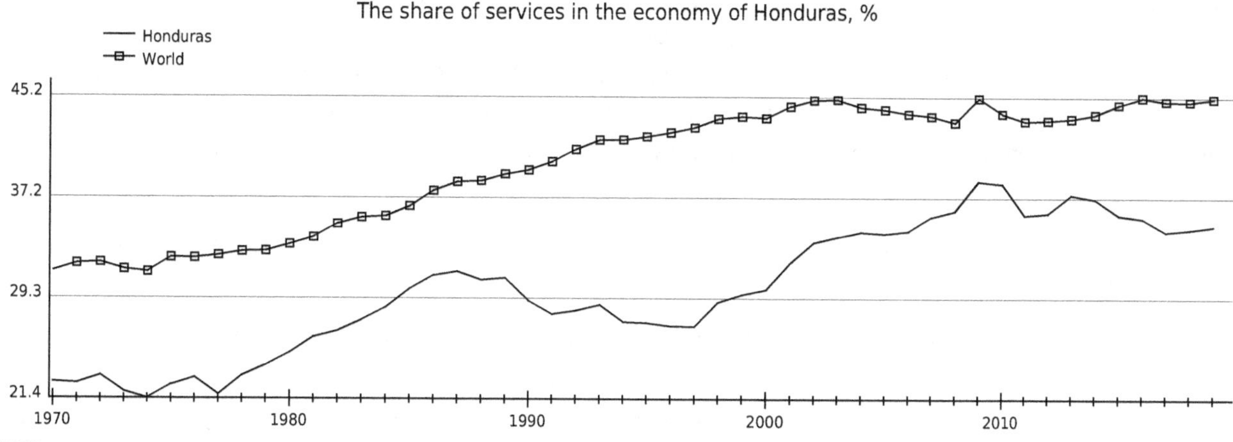

The 1970s

The value of services in Honduras was $337.5 million per year in the 1970s, ranked 104th in the world, and was on a par with French Polynesia ($334.3 million), El Salvador ($333.1 million). The share in the world was 0.016%, and 0.040% in the Americas.

The share of services in the economy of Honduras was 22.8% in the 1970s, ranked 128th in the world.

The Honduran services per capita were $108.2 in the 1970s, ranked 132nd in the world. The value of services per capita in Honduras was less than services per capita in the world ($506.9) in 4.7 times, and was less than services per capita in the Americas ($1 502.8) in 13.9 times.

The growth of services in Honduras was 8.8% in the 1970s, ranked 29th in the world. The growth of services in Honduras (8.8%) was greater than growth of services in the world (4.1%), was greater than growth of services in the Americas (3.7%).

Comparison with neighbors. The sector of services in Honduras was greater than in El Salvador ($333.1 million); but less than in Guatemala ($1.1 billion) and in Nicaragua ($699.2 million). The Honduran services per capita were greater than in El Salvador ($81.2); but less than in Nicaragua ($252.0) and in Guatemala ($172.7). The growth of services in Honduras was greater than in Guatemala (5.3%), in El Salvador (4.8%), and in Nicaragua (-1.5%).

Comparison with leaders. The sector of services in Honduras was less than in the USA ($674.4 billion), in the USSR ($168.3 billion), in Japan ($153.8 billion), in Germany ($150.2 billion), and in France ($121.8 billion). The Honduras services per capita were less than in the United States ($3.1 thousand), in France ($2.3 thousand), in Germany ($1 907.6), in Japan ($1 381.3), and in the USSR ($667.3). The growth of services in Honduras was greater than in Japan (5.9%), in Germany (4.8%), in France (3.9%), in the USA (3.3%), and in the USSR (0.90%).

The 1980s

The value of services in Honduras was $1.2 billion per year in the 1980s, ranked 90th in the world, and was on a par with Jamaica ($1.2 billion). The share in the world was 0.023%, and 0.054% in the Americas.

The share of services in the economy of Honduras was 29.3% in the 1980s, ranked 99th in the world, and was on a par with Trinidad and Tobago (29.2%), Kuwait (29.4%), Congo (29.1%).

The Honduras services per capita were $293.7 in the 1980s, ranked 113th in the world, and were on a par with Western Africa ($295.8), Syria ($300.5), Djibouti ($300.6). The sector of services per capita in Honduras was less than services per capita in the world ($1 115.5) in 3.8 times, and was less than services per capita in the Americas ($3 456.8) in 11.8 times.

The growth of services in Honduras was 3.3% in the 1980s, ranked 95th in the world, and was on a par with South Africa (3.3%), the United Kingdom (3.3%), the World (3.3%). The growth of services in Honduras (3.3%) was greater than growth of services in the world (3.3%), was greater than growth of services in the Americas (2.8%).

Comparison with neighbors. The Honduran services were greater than in El Salvador ($1.0 billion) and in Nicaragua ($935.3 million); but less than in Guatemala ($2.5 billion). The sector of services per capita in Honduras was greater than in Nicaragua ($254.1) and in El Salvador ($212.9); but less than in Guatemala ($311.1). The growth of services in Honduras was greater than in Guatemala (2.1%), in El Salvador (1.7%), and in Nicaragua (0.012%).

Comparison with leaders. The value added of services in Honduras was less than in the United States ($1.9 trillion), in Japan ($619.9 billion), in Germany ($362.2 billion), in France ($294.5 billion), and in the United Kingdom ($265.4 billion). The value added of services per capita in Honduras was less than in the USA ($7.8 thousand), in France ($5.2 thousand), in Japan ($5.1 thousand), in the United Kingdom ($4.7 thousand), and in Germany ($4.6 thousand). The growth of services in Honduras was greater than in the United Kingdom (3.3%), in Germany (3.1%), in the United States (2.8%), and in France (2.3%); but less than in Japan (4.8%).

The 1990s

The value of services in Honduras was $1.3 billion per year in the 1990s, ranked 119th in the world. The share in the world was 0.011%, and 0.026% in the Americas.

The share of services in the economy of Honduras was 28.3% in the 1990s, ranked 129th in the world, and was on a par with Trinidad and Tobago (28.3%), Rwanda (28.4%).

The sector of services per capita in Honduras was $223.3 in the 1990s, ranked 143rd in the world. The sector of services per capita in Honduras was less than services per capita in the world ($2 014.6) in 9.0 times, and was less than services per capita in the Americas ($6 173.1) in 27.6 times.

The growth of services in Honduras was 2.7% in the 1990s, ranked 113th in the world, and was on a par with Benin (2.7%), the World (2.7%), Northern Europe (2.7%). The growth of services in Honduras (2.7%) was less than growth of services in the world (2.7%), was greater than growth of services in the Americas (2.4%).

Comparison with neighbors. The value of services in Honduras was greater than in Nicaragua ($1.1 billion); but less than in Guatemala ($4.2 billion) and in El Salvador ($2.5 billion). The sector of services per capita in Honduras was less than in El Salvador ($453.1), in Guatemala ($405.1), and in Nicaragua ($249.1). The growth of services in Honduras was greater than in Nicaragua (1.7%); but less than in El Salvador (7.8%) and in Guatemala (4.4%).

Comparison with leaders. The value of services in Honduras was less than in the USA ($3.8 trillion), in Japan ($1.6 trillion), in Germany ($908.0 billion), in France ($628.2 billion), and in the UK ($592.3 billion). The value added of services per capita in Honduras was less than in the United States ($14.4 thousand), in Japan ($12.8 thousand), in Germany ($11.3 thousand), in France ($10.6 thousand), and in the UK ($10.2 thousand). The growth of services in Honduras was greater than in the United States (2.3%), in Japan (1.7%), and in France (1.6%); but less than in Germany (3.2%) and in the UK (3.0%).

The 2000s

The value added of services in Honduras was $3.4 billion per year in the 2000s, ranked 105th in the world, and was on a par with Turkmenistan ($3.4 billion). The share in the world was 0.017%, and 0.041% in the Americas.

The share of services in the economy of Honduras was 34.9% in the 2000s, ranked 104th in the world, and was on a par with Vanuatu (34.9%), Botswana (35.1%), the Maldives (34.8%).

The sector of services per capita in Honduras was $460.3 in the 2000s, ranked 139th in the world, and was on a par with Algeria ($456.5). The Honduran services per capita were less than services per capita in the world ($3 011.2) in 6.5 times, and were less than services per capita in the Americas ($9 407.5) in 20.4 times.

The growth of services in Honduras was 7.8% in the 2000s, ranked 24th in the world. The growth of services in Honduras (7.8%) was greater than growth of services in the world (2.9%), was greater than growth of services in the Americas (2.2%).

Comparison with neighbors. The services of Honduras were greater than in Nicaragua ($2.1 billion); but less than in Guatemala ($9.2 billion) and in El Salvador ($5.3 billion). The Honduras services per capita were greater than in Nicaragua ($387.4); but less than in El Salvador ($885.8) and in Guatemala ($709.7). The growth of services in Honduras was greater than in Guatemala (3.9%), in Nicaragua (3.5%), and in El Salvador (3.0%).

Comparison with leaders. The sector of services in Honduras was less than in the USA ($6.7 trillion), in Japan ($2.0 trillion), in Germany ($1.2 trillion), in the UK ($1.1 trillion), and in France ($997.0 billion). The value added of services per capita in Honduras was less than in the USA ($22.9 thousand), in the UK ($18.0 thousand), in France ($15.9 thousand), in Japan ($15.3 thousand), and in Germany ($15.0 thousand). The growth of services in Honduras was greater than in the UK (2.7%), in the United States (2.0%), in France (1.5%), in Japan (1.2%), and in Germany (0.57%).

The 2010s

The Honduras services were $7.2 billion per year in the 2010s, ranked 103rd in the world. The share in the world was 0.022%, and 0.056% in the Americas.

The share of services in the economy of Honduras was 36.0% in the 2010s, ranked 100th in the world, and was on a par with Cabo Verde (35.9%), the Maldives (35.9%), Tunisia (35.8%).

The value added of services per capita in Honduras was $792.4 in the 2010s, ranked 147th in the world, and was on a par with Egypt ($787.3). The value of services per capita in Honduras was less than services per capita in the world ($4 467.8) in 5.6 times, and was less than services per capita in the Americas ($13 184.6) in 16.6 times.

The growth of services in Honduras was 4.4% in the 2010s, ranked 72nd in the world, and was on a par with the Maldives (4.4%). The growth of services in Honduras (4.4%) was greater than growth of services in the world (2.7%), was greater than growth of services in the Americas (1.8%).

Comparison with neighbors. The Honduras services were 2.1 times higher than in Nicaragua ($3.5 billion); but 2.8 times lower than in Guatemala ($19.7 billion) and 16.7% lower than in El Salvador ($8.6 billion). The sector of services per capita in Honduras was 41.1% higher than in Nicaragua ($561.6); but 41.8% lower than in El Salvador ($1 360.5) and 35.4% lower than in Guatemala ($1 226.9). The growth of services in Honduras was greater than in Guatemala (4.2%), in Nicaragua (2.6%), and in El Salvador (1.9%).

Comparison with leaders. The Honduran services were 1 390.7 times lower than in the USA ($10.0 trillion), 495.5 times lower than in China ($3.5 trillion), 317.6 times lower than in Japan ($2.3 trillion), 224.6 times lower than in Germany ($1.6 trillion), and 189.4 times lower than in the United Kingdom ($1.4 trillion). The services per capita in Honduras were 39.3 times lower than in the USA ($31.2 thousand), 26.1 times lower than in the United Kingdom ($20.7 thousand), 24.8 times lower than in Germany ($19.6 thousand), 22.4 times lower than in Japan ($17.8 thousand), and 3.2 times lower than in China ($2.5 thousand). The growth of services in Honduras was greater than in the United States (1.8%), in the UK (1.7%), in Germany (1.2%), and in Japan (0.99%); but less than China (8.4%).

Part III. External relations

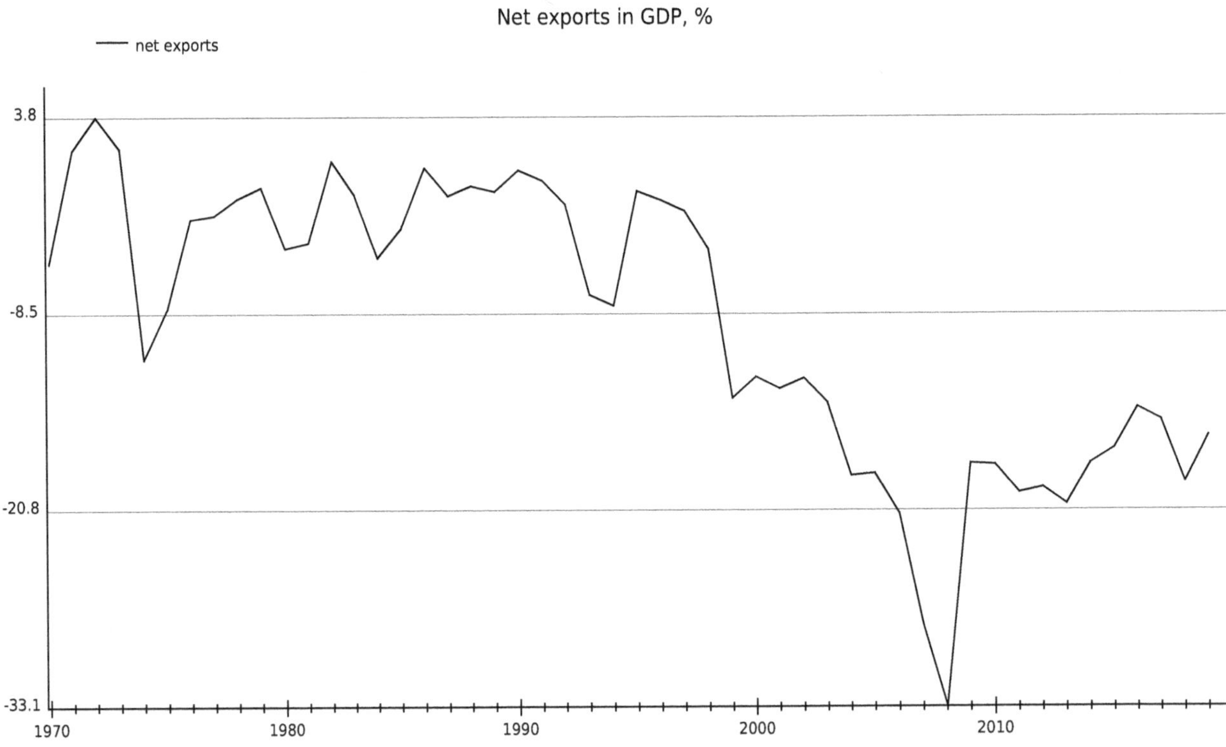

Chapter X. Exports

Exports of goods and services

The exports of Honduras enlarged from $649.2 million per year in the 1970s to $9.3 billion per year in the 2010s, that is by $8.6 billion or 14.3 times. The change occurred at $7.4 billion due to a 4.9-fold increase in prices, as also at $11.6 million due to a 1.0-fold increase in per capita rate, as well as at $1.2 billion due to the increase in population. The average annual growth in exports is 2.9%. The minimum value of exports was in 1970 at $307.6 million. The maximum value of exports was in 2019 at $10.1 billion.

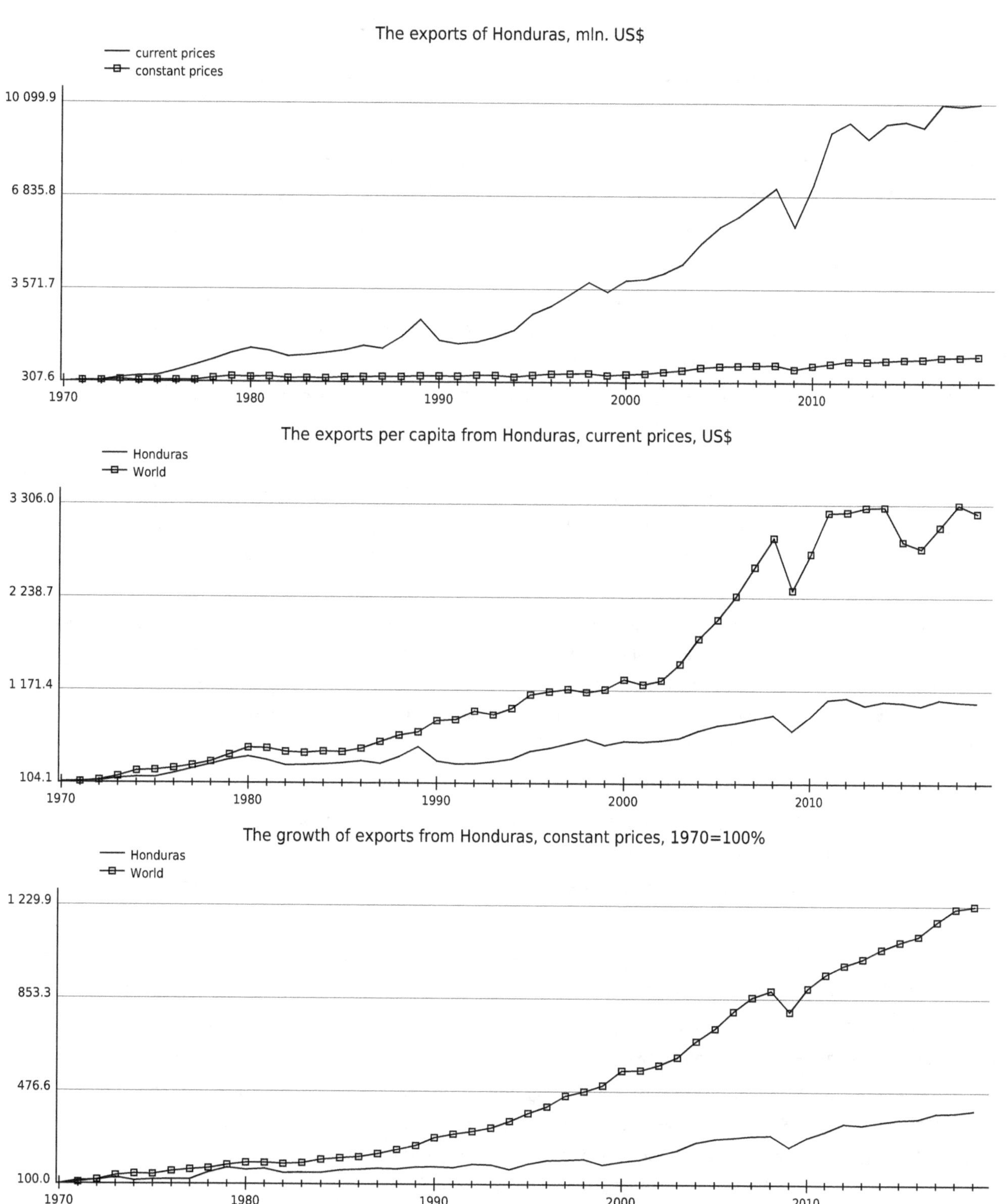

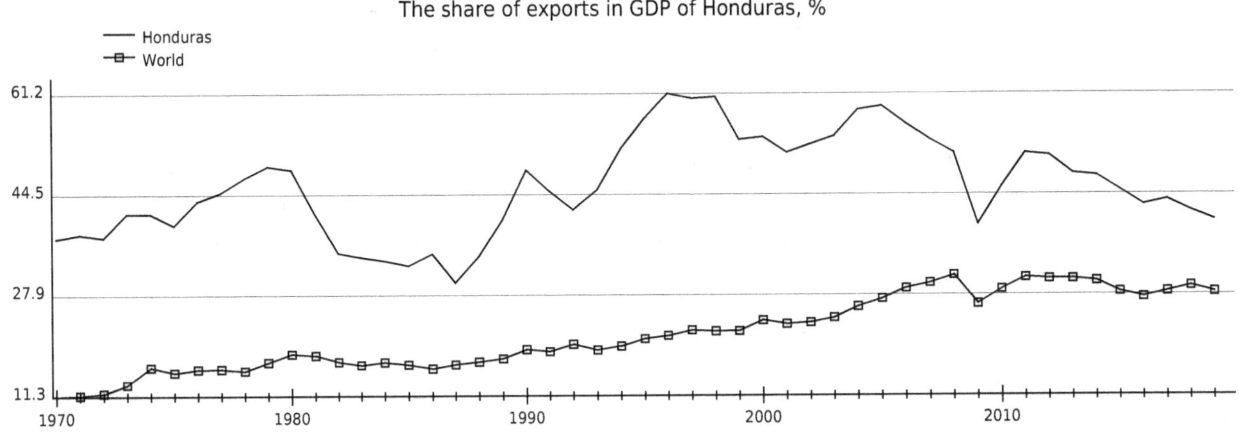

The 1970s

The exports of Honduras were $649.2 million per year in the 1970s, ranked 86th in the world, and were on a par with Namibia ($643.2 million), Cyprus ($634.8 million). The share in the world was 0.066%, and 0.29% from the Americas.

The share of exports in GDP of Honduras was 43.6% in the 1970s, ranked 52nd in the world, and was on a par with Liechtenstein (43.5%), Switzerland (43.2%).

The exports per capita from Honduras were $208.1 in the 1970s, ranked 102nd in the world, and were on a par with Northern Africa ($207.6), Tunisia ($211.1), Uruguay ($204.6). The Honduras exports per capita were less than exports per capita in the world ($242.1) by 14.0%, and were less than exports per capita from the Americas ($397.2) by 47.6%.

The growth of exports from Honduras was 5.8% in the 1970s, ranked 92nd in the world, and was on a par with Finland (5.8%), the Comoros (5.8%). The growth of exports from Honduras (5.8%) was less than growth of exports in the world (6.5%), was less than growth of exports from the Americas (6.4%).

Comparison with neighbors. The value of exports from Honduras was greater than from Nicaragua ($412.1 million) and from El Salvador ($212.8 million); but less than from Guatemala ($999.7 million). The Honduras exports per capita were greater than from Guatemala ($157.3), from Nicaragua ($148.5), and from El Salvador ($51.9). The growth of exports from Honduras was less than from El Salvador (7.5%), from Nicaragua (6.7%), and from Guatemala (6.7%).

Comparison with leaders. The exports of Honduras were less than from the United States ($128.0 billion), from Germany ($82.9 billion), from France ($64.3 billion), from Japan ($64.1 billion), and from the United Kingdom ($61.3 billion). The value of exports per capita from Honduras was less than from France ($1 199.1), from the United Kingdom ($1 094.1), from Germany ($1 052.2), from the United States ($586.5), and from Japan ($575.8). The growth of exports from Honduras was greater than from Germany (5.1%) and from the United Kingdom (5.0%); but less than from Japan (8.6%), from France (7.8%), and from the United States (6.8%).

The 1980s

The Honduras exports were $1.6 billion per year in the 1980s, ranked 84th in the world, and were on a par with Sri Lanka ($1.6 billion). The share in the world was 0.061%, and 0.26% from the Americas.

The share of exports in GDP of Honduras was 36.1% in the 1980s, ranked 68th in the world, and was on a par with Côte d'Ivoire (36.4%).

The Honduras exports per capita were $367.4 in the 1980s, ranked 103rd in the world. The exports per capita from Honduras were less than exports per capita in the world ($529.9) by 30.7%, and were less than exports per capita from the Americas ($890.9) in 2.4 times.

The growth of exports from Honduras was 0.2% in the 1980s, ranked 145th in the world. The growth of exports from Honduras (0.24%) was less than growth of exports in the world (3.8%), was less than growth of exports from the Americas (5.1%).

Comparison with neighbors. The value of exports from Honduras was greater than from El Salvador ($440.6 million) and from Nicaragua ($376.9 million); but less than from Guatemala ($1.7 billion). The Honduran exports per capita were greater than from Guatemala ($212.7), from Nicaragua ($102.4), and from El Salvador ($89.9). The growth of exports from Honduras was greater than from Guatemala (-2.2%), from El Salvador (-6.5%), and from Nicaragua (-7.5%).

Comparison with leaders. The exports of Honduras were less than from the United States ($338.6 billion), from Japan ($210.6 billion), from Germany ($208.1 billion), from France ($155.9 billion), and from the UK ($155.0 billion). The value of exports per capita from Honduras was less than from France ($2.8 thousand), from the UK ($2.7 thousand), from Germany ($2.7 thousand), from Japan ($1 736.5), and from the USA ($1 413.8). The growth of exports from Honduras was less than from Japan (6.7%), from the United States (5.7%), from Germany (4.7%), from France (4.0%), and from the UK (3.0%).

The 1990s

The Honduran exports were $2.5 billion per year in the 1990s, ranked 98th in the world, and were on a par with DR Congo ($2.5 billion), Kenya ($2.5 billion), San Marino ($2.5 billion). The share in the world was 0.043%, and 0.20% from the Americas.

The share of exports in GDP of Honduras was 53.5% in the 1990s, ranked 35th in the world, and was on a par with Slovenia (53.5%), Papua New Guinea (53.3%), Belarus (53.2%).

The exports per capita from Honduras were $451.3 in the 1990s, ranked 117th in the world, and were on a par with Lebanon ($453.0), Asia ($456.7), Algeria ($441.0). The Honduran exports per capita were less than exports per capita in the world ($1 029.5) in 2.3 times, and were less than exports per capita from the Americas ($1 662.5) in 3.7 times.

The growth of exports from Honduras was 0.6% in the 1990s, ranked 164th in the world. The growth of exports from Honduras (0.59%) was less than growth of exports in the world (6.9%), was less than growth of exports from the Americas (7.3%).

Comparison with neighbors. The value of exports from Honduras was greater than from El Salvador ($1.8 billion) and from Nicaragua ($717.7 million); but less than from Guatemala ($3.1 billion). The exports per capita from Honduras were greater than from El Salvador ($315.3), from Guatemala ($298.4), and from Nicaragua ($156.2). The growth of exports from Honduras was less than from El Salvador (14.7%), from Nicaragua (9.3%), and from Guatemala (5.8%).

Comparison with leaders. The Honduran exports were less than from the USA ($773.6 billion), from Germany ($509.0 billion), from Japan ($418.7 billion), from France ($329.8 billion), and from the United Kingdom ($324.3 billion). The exports per capita from Honduras were less than from Germany ($6.3 thousand), from the UK ($5.6 thousand), from France ($5.6 thousand), from Japan ($3.3 thousand), and from the USA ($2.9 thousand). The growth of exports from Honduras was less than from the USA (7.2%), from France (6.5%), from Germany (6.0%), from the United Kingdom (5.7%), and from Japan (4.2%).

The 2000s

The exports of Honduras were $5.3 billion per year in the 2000s, ranked 101st in the world, and were on a par with Paraguay ($5.3 billion), Papua New Guinea ($5.3 billion), Sudan ($5.3 billion). The share in the world was 0.042%, and 0.22% from the Americas.

The structure of exports: primary products (26.6%), resource-based manufactures (14.2%), low technology manufactures (46.5%), and medium technology manufactures (8.5%).

Honduras exported goods to the United States (65.4%), El Salvador (5.5%), Guatemala (4.0%), Germany (3.7%), Belgium (2.4%) and other countries (19.0%).

The share of exports in GDP of Honduras was 52.3% in the 2000s, ranked 55th in the world, and was on a par with Middle Africa (52.3%), Lesotho (52.1%), Lithuania (51.9%).

The Honduras exports per capita were $719.0 in the 2000s, ranked 129th in the world, and were on a par with Peru ($724.8). The exports per capita from Honduras were less than exports per capita in the world ($1 933.7) in 2.7 times, and were less than exports per capita from the Americas ($2 781.7) in 3.9 times.

The growth of exports from Honduras was 3.5% in the 2000s, ranked 124th in the world, and was on a par with the Netherlands (3.4%). The growth of exports from Honduras (3.5%) was less than growth of exports in the world (4.8%), was greater than growth of exports from the Americas (2.9%).

Comparison with neighbors. The Honduras exports were greater than from El Salvador ($3.8 billion) and from Nicaragua ($1.8 billion); but less than from Guatemala ($6.4 billion). The value of exports per capita from Honduras was greater than from El Salvador ($624.9), from Guatemala ($492.0), and from Nicaragua ($340.4). The growth of exports from Honduras was greater than from El Salvador (3.2%) and from Guatemala (1.7%); but less than from Nicaragua (7.9%).

Comparison with leaders. The exports of Honduras were less than from the United States ($1.3 trillion), from Germany ($1.0 trillion), from China ($780.2 billion), from Japan ($626.3 billion), and from the UK ($591.1 billion). The exports per capita from Honduras were greater than from China ($588.1); but less than from Germany ($12.8 thousand), from the UK ($9.8 thousand), from Japan ($4.9 thousand), and from the United States ($4.5 thousand). The growth of exports from Honduras was greater than from the United States (3.3%) and from the UK (2.8%); but less than from China (12.7%), from Germany (5.0%), and from Japan (3.5%).

The 2010s

The exports of Honduras were $9.3 billion per year in the 2010s, ranked 106th in the world, and were on a par with Brunei ($9.3 billion), Zambia ($9.2 billion), Iceland ($9.5 billion). The share in the world was 0.041%, and 0.23% from the Americas.

The structure of exports: primary products (33.5%), resource-based manufactures (17.3%), low technology manufactures (31.3%), and medium technology manufactures (12.8%).

Honduras exported goods to the United States (50.0%), El Salvador (6.5%), Germany (6.4%), Guatemala (4.6%), Mexico (4.0%) and other countries (28.5%).

The share of exports in GDP of Honduras was 45.3% in the 2010s, ranked 75th in the world, and was on a par with Republic of Korea (45.4%), Tunisia (45.6%).

The Honduras exports per capita were $1 029.3 in the 2010s, ranked 142nd in the world. The exports per capita from Honduras were less than exports per capita in the world ($3 098.9) in 3.0 times, and were less than exports per capita from the Americas ($4 197.2) in 4.1 times.

The growth of exports from Honduras was 4.8% in the 2010s, ranked 82nd in the world, and was on a par with Bahrain (4.7%), Anguilla (4.7%), the Netherlands (4.8%). The growth of exports from Honduras (4.8%) was greater than growth of exports in the world (4.4%), was greater than growth of exports from the Americas (3.6%).

Comparison with neighbors. The Honduran exports were 39.4% higher than from El Salvador ($6.7 billion) and 84.5% higher than from Nicaragua ($5.0 billion); but 23.7% lower than from Guatemala ($12.2 billion). The Honduran exports per capita were 26.3% higher than from Nicaragua ($814.8) and 36.0% higher than from Guatemala ($757.1); but 2.6% lower than from El Salvador ($1 056.8). The growth of exports from Honduras was greater than from El Salvador (3.2%) and from Guatemala (3.0%); but less than from Nicaragua (6.4%).

Comparison with leaders. The value of exports from Honduras was 246.6 times lower than from China ($2.3 trillion), 244.1 times lower than from the USA ($2.3 trillion), 181.0 times lower than from Germany ($1.7 trillion), 92.4 times lower than from Japan ($859.4 billion), and 87.7 times lower than from the UK ($815.1 billion). The exports per capita from Honduras were 20.0 times lower than from Germany ($20.6 thousand), 12.1 times lower than from the United Kingdom ($12.4 thousand), 6.9 times lower than from the USA ($7.1 thousand), 6.5 times lower than from Japan ($6.7 thousand), and 37.1% lower than from China ($1 635.3). The growth of exports from Honduras was greater than from Germany (4.7%), from Japan (4.6%), from the USA (3.7%), and from the UK (3.1%); but less than from China (6.8%).

Chapter XI. Imports

Imports of goods and services

The Honduran imports grew up from $684.4 million per year in the 1970s to $12.9 billion per year in the 2010s, that is by $12.2 billion or 18.9 times. The change occurred at $10.6 billion due to a 5.5-fold increase in prices, as also at $343.4 million due to a 1.2-fold increase in per capita rate, as well as at $1.3 billion due to the growth in population. The average annual growth in imports is 3.0%. The minimum value of imports was in 1971 at $316.4 million. The maximum value of imports was in 2018 at $14.6 billion.

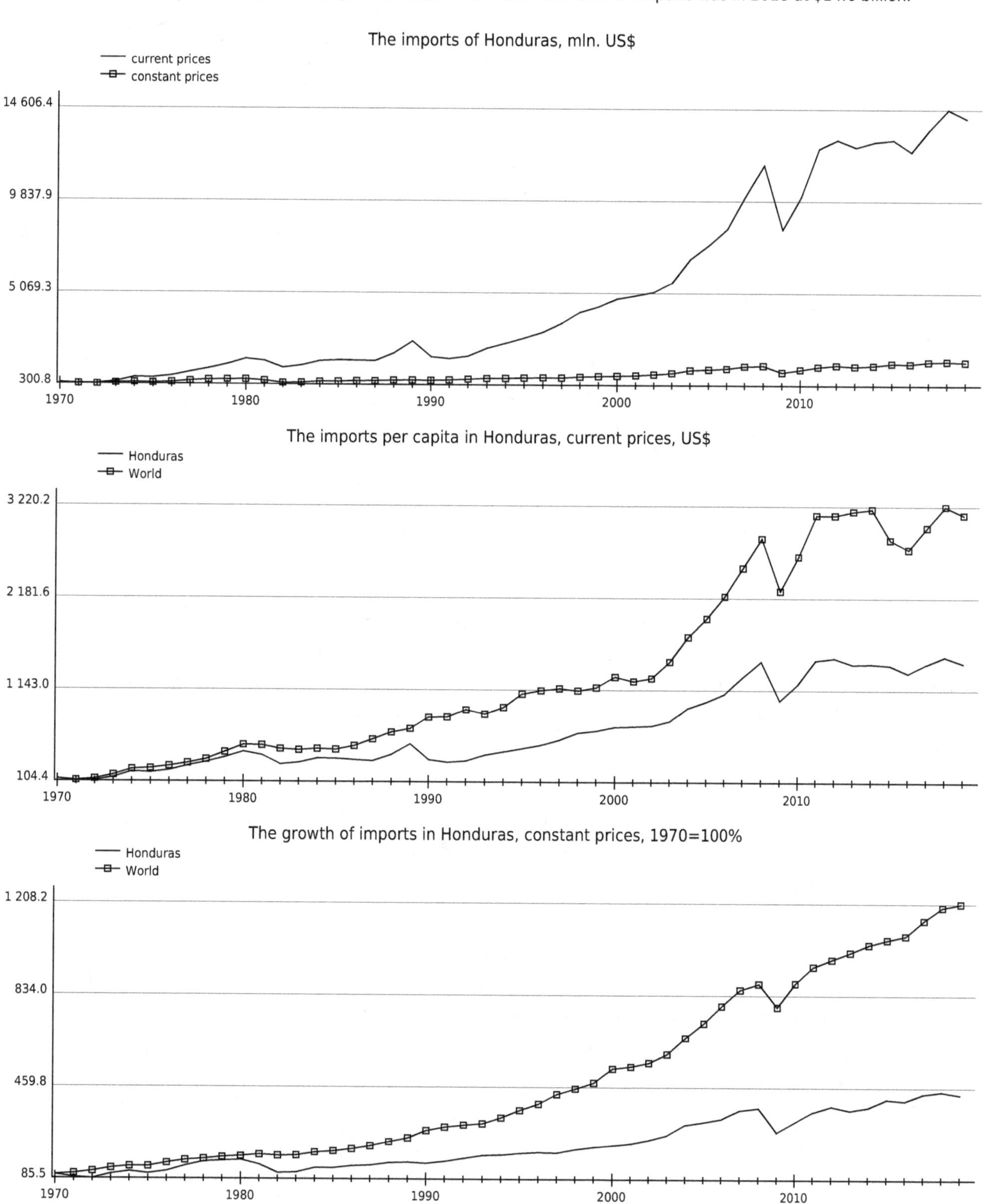

The 1970s

The imports of Honduras were $684.4 million per year in the 1970s, ranked 89th in the world, and were on a par with Uganda ($680.7 million), Oman ($679.4 million). The share in the world was 0.069%, and 0.29% in the Americas.

The share of imports in GDP of Honduras was 45.9% in the 1970s, ranked 59th in the world, and was on a par with Trinidad and Tobago (45.6%).

The value of imports per capita in Honduras was $219.4 in the 1970s, ranked 115th in the world, and was on a par with Syria ($220.0), Angola ($218.0), Mauritania ($221.0). The value of imports per capita in Honduras was less than imports per capita in the world ($244.3) by 10.2%, and was less than imports per capita in the Americas ($421.7) by 48.0%.

The growth of imports in Honduras was 5.2% in the 1970s, ranked 104th in the world, and was on a par with Suriname (5.2%), South America (5.2%). The growth of imports in Honduras (5.2%) was less than growth of imports in the world (6.3%), was less than growth of imports in the Americas (5.4%).

Comparison with neighbors. The imports of Honduras were greater than in Nicaragua ($393.1 million) and in El Salvador ($231.7 million); but less than in Guatemala ($1.2 billion). The imports per capita in Honduras were greater than in Guatemala ($183.8), in Nicaragua ($141.7), and in El Salvador ($56.5). The growth of imports in Honduras was greater than in Nicaragua (0.72%); but less than in El Salvador (8.3%) and in Guatemala (5.7%).

Comparison with leaders. The value of imports in Honduras was less than in the United States ($133.2 billion), in Germany ($92.5 billion), in France ($63.3 billion), in the UK ($62.4 billion), and in Japan ($61.0 billion). The Honduran imports per capita were less than in France ($1 181.1), in Germany ($1 175.1), in the United Kingdom ($1 113.2), in the United States ($610.4), and in Japan ($547.6). The growth of imports in Honduras was greater than in the USA (5.1%) and in the United Kingdom (4.5%); but less than in France (7.2%), in Japan (7.0%), and in Germany (5.6%).

The 1980s

The Honduras imports were $1.6 billion per year in the 1980s, ranked 86th in the world, and were on a par with Malta ($1.6 billion), Gabon ($1.6 billion), Uruguay ($1.6 billion). The share in the world was 0.062%, and 0.25% in the Americas.

The share of imports in GDP of Honduras was 37.7% in the 1980s, ranked 81st in the world, and was on a par with Middle Africa (37.6%), South-Eastern Asia (38.1%).

The value of imports per capita in Honduras was $384.1 in the 1980s, ranked 114th in the world, and was on a par with Romania ($386.5), Mexico ($381.1), Central America ($387.4). The imports per capita in Honduras were less than imports per capita in the world ($539.1) by 28.7%, and were less than imports per capita in the Americas ($984.9) in 2.6 times.

The growth of imports in Honduras was -0.3% in the 1980s, ranked 145th in the world. The growth of imports in Honduras (-0.31%) was less than growth of imports in the world (3.8%), was less than growth of imports in the Americas (3.8%).

Comparison with neighbors. The Honduran imports were greater than in Nicaragua ($636.9 million) and in El Salvador ($586.6 million); but less than in Guatemala ($2.1 billion). The value of imports per capita in Honduras was greater than in Guatemala ($261.1), in Nicaragua ($173.0), and in El Salvador ($119.7). The growth of imports in Honduras was greater than in Guatemala (-3.3%) and in El

Salvador (-4.3%); but less than in Nicaragua (2.4%).

Comparison with leaders. The value of imports in Honduras was less than in the United States ($417.2 billion), in Germany ($225.6 billion), in Japan ($175.9 billion), in France ($162.0 billion), and in the UK ($157.7 billion). The Honduran imports per capita were less than in Germany ($2.9 thousand), in France ($2.9 thousand), in the UK ($2.8 thousand), in the USA ($1 742.4), and in Japan ($1 450.4). The growth of imports in Honduras was less than in the USA (5.8%), in the UK (5.1%), in Japan (4.6%), in France (4.3%), and in Germany (3.3%).

The 1990s

The Honduras imports were $2.8 billion per year in the 1990s, ranked 100th in the world. The share in the world was 0.048%, and 0.20% in the Americas.

The share of imports in GDP of Honduras was 57.9% in the 1990s, ranked 50th in the world, and was on a par with Belgium (57.9%).

The imports per capita in Honduras were $488.0 in the 1990s, ranked 133rd in the world, and were on a par with South America ($481.6), Cuba ($495.2). The Honduran imports per capita were less than imports per capita in the world ($1 015.5) in 2.1 times, and were less than imports per capita in the Americas ($1 812.7) in 3.7 times.

The growth of imports in Honduras was 3.5% in the 1990s, ranked 122nd in the world, and was on a par with Switzerland (3.5%), Papua New Guinea (3.5%). The growth of imports in Honduras (3.5%) was less than growth of imports in the world (6.6%), was less than growth of imports in the Americas (8.2%).

Comparison with neighbors. The Honduras imports were greater than in Nicaragua ($1.4 billion); but less than in Guatemala ($4.3 billion) and in El Salvador ($2.9 billion). The value of imports per capita in Honduras was greater than in Guatemala ($417.4) and in Nicaragua ($312.7); but less than in El Salvador ($512.4). The growth of imports in Honduras was less than in Nicaragua (10.5%), in El Salvador (10.0%), and in Guatemala (9.1%).

Comparison with leaders. The value of imports in Honduras was less than in the USA ($874.1 billion), in Germany ($501.6 billion), in Japan ($355.9 billion), in the UK ($330.2 billion), and in France ($308.5 billion). The Honduran imports per capita were less than in Germany ($6.2 thousand), in the United Kingdom ($5.7 thousand), in France ($5.2 thousand), in the USA ($3.3 thousand), and in Japan ($2.8 thousand). The growth of imports in Honduras was greater than in Japan (3.3%); but less than in the United States (8.3%), in Germany (6.4%), in France (5.1%), and in the UK (5.1%).

The 2000s

The imports of Honduras were $7.3 billion per year in the 2000s, ranked 89th in the world, and were on a par with Bosnia and Herzegovina ($7.3 billion). The share in the world was 0.059%, and 0.25% in the Americas.

The structure of imports: primary products (8.6%), resource-based manufactures (25.1%), low technology manufactures (28.4%), medium technology manufactures (24.8%), and high technology manufactures (9.3%).

Honduras imported goods from the USA (54.3%), Guatemala (6.3%), El Salvador (5.1%), Mexico (4.2%), Panama (2.6%) and other countries (27.6%).

The share of imports in GDP of Honduras was 72.5% in the 2000s, ranked 29th in the world, and was on a par with Vietnam (72.6%), Ireland (72.9%), Guyana (72.0%).

The imports per capita in Honduras were $996.7 in the 2000s, ranked 127th in the world, and were on a par with Vanuatu ($1 014.3), Angola ($977.0). The imports per capita in Honduras were less than imports per capita in the world ($1 899.9) by 47.5%, and were less than imports per capita in the Americas ($3 354.4) in 3.4 times.

The growth of imports in Honduras was 2.6% in the 2000s, ranked 162nd in the world, and was on a par with Southern Europe (2.6%). The growth of imports in Honduras (2.6%) was less than growth of imports in the world (5.1%), was less than growth of imports in the Americas (3.5%).

Comparison with neighbors. The Honduras imports were greater than in El Salvador ($6.7 billion) and in Nicaragua ($3.4 billion); but less than in Guatemala ($10.6 billion). The imports per capita in Honduras were greater than in Guatemala ($818.1) and in Nicaragua ($622.7); but less than in El Salvador ($1 107.5). The growth of imports in Honduras was greater than in El Salvador (2.3%) and in Guatemala (1.9%); but less than in Nicaragua (3.2%).

Comparison with leaders. The value of imports in Honduras was less than in the United States ($1.9 trillion), in Germany ($914.7 billion), in the United Kingdom ($641.8 billion), in China ($641.1 billion), and in Japan ($566.4 billion). The imports per capita in Honduras were greater than in China ($483.3); but less than in Germany ($11.2 thousand), in the United Kingdom ($10.6 thousand), in the USA ($6.4 thousand), and in Japan ($4.4 thousand). The growth of imports in Honduras was greater than in Japan (1.8%); but less than in China (15.1%), in Germany (3.7%), in the UK (3.1%), and in the United States (2.8%).

The 2010s

The Honduran imports were $12.9 billion per year in the 2010s, ranked 97th in the world, and were on a par with Cuba ($13.1 billion). The share in the world was 0.058%, and 0.27% in the Americas.

The structure of imports: primary products (9.4%), resource-based manufactures (30.2%), low technology manufactures (23.2%), medium technology manufactures (23.4%), and high technology manufactures (10.7%).

Honduras imported goods from the USA (51.2%), Guatemala (7.4%), China (7.1%), El Salvador (5.8%), Mexico (5.4%) and other countries (23.1%).

The share of imports in GDP of Honduras was 62.8% in the 2010s, ranked 47th in the world, and was on a par with Tonga (62.9%), Belize (62.7%), Cape Verde (62.3%).

The value of imports per capita in Honduras was $1 428.1 in the 2010s, ranked 144th in the world, and was on a par with Colombia ($1 431.2), Morocco ($1 447.0), Brazil ($1 395.6). The imports per capita in Honduras were less than imports per capita in the world ($3 015.6) in 2.1 times, and were less than imports per capita in the Americas ($4 884.3) in 3.4 times.

The growth of imports in Honduras was 4.5% in the 2010s, ranked 91st in the world, and was on a par with Indonesia (4.5%), Papua New Guinea (4.5%), Sweden (4.5%). The growth of imports in Honduras (4.5%) was greater than growth of imports in the world (4.4%), was greater than growth of imports in the Americas (3.3%).

Comparison with neighbors. The value of imports in Honduras was 17.3% higher than in El Salvador ($11.0 billion) and 87.7% higher than in Nicaragua ($6.9 billion); but 31.1% lower than in Guatemala ($18.7 billion). The value of imports per capita in Honduras was 22.8% higher than in Guatemala ($1 162.8) and 28.5% higher than in Nicaragua ($1 111.6); but 18.0% lower than in El Salvador ($1 742.4). The growth of imports in Honduras was greater than in Guatemala (4.4%), in Nicaragua (3.3%), and in El Salvador (3.2%).

Comparison with leaders. The value of imports in Honduras was 218.4 times lower than in the United States ($2.8 trillion), 160.4 times lower than in China ($2.1 trillion), 112.8 times lower than in Germany ($1.5 trillion), 68.0 times lower than in Japan ($877.9 billion), and 66.3 times lower than in the United Kingdom ($854.8 billion). The value of imports per capita in Honduras was 12.4 times lower than in Germany ($17.8 thousand), 9.1 times lower than in the United Kingdom ($13.0 thousand), 6.2 times lower than in the United States ($8.8 thousand), 4.8 times lower than in Japan ($6.9 thousand), and 3.2% lower than in China ($1 475.4). The growth of imports in Honduras was greater than in the United States (4.4%), in Japan (3.8%), and in the UK (3.6%); but less than in China (8.2%) and in Germany (4.8%).

Part IV. Consumption

Chapter XII. Government consumption expenditure

General government final consumption expenditure

The Honduran government expenditure rose from $185.8 million per year in the 1970s to $3.1 billion per year in the 2010s, that is by $2.9 billion or 16.5 times. The change occurred at $2.3 billion due to a 4.2-fold increase in prices, as also at $190.5 million due to a 1.4-fold increase in per capita rate, as well as at $352.2 million due to the growing in population. The average annual growth in public expenditure is 3.5%. The minimum value of government consumption expenditure was in 1970 at $105.8 million. The maximum value of government consumption expenditure was in 2019 at $3.4 billion.

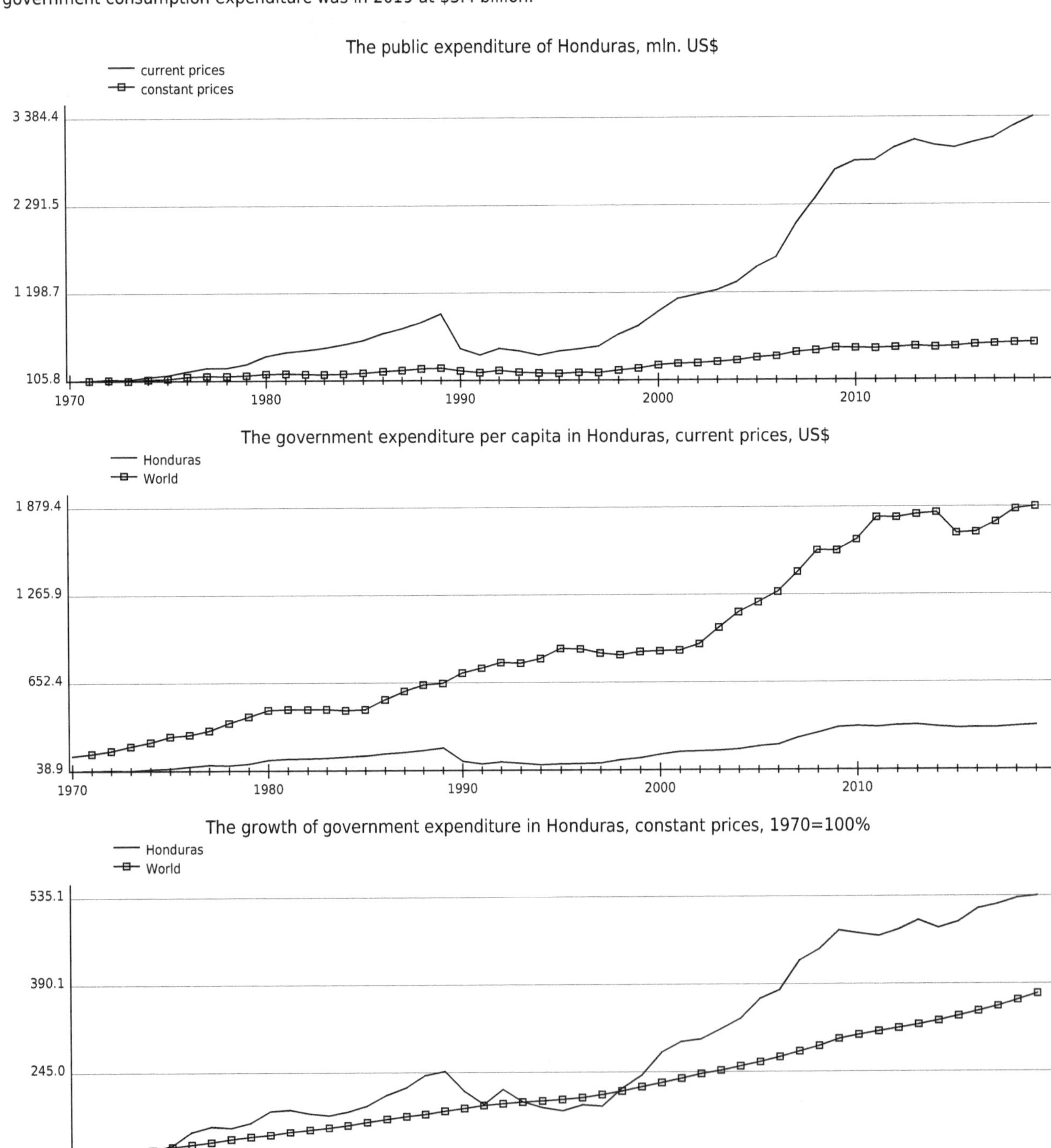

The public expenditure of Honduras, mln. US$

The government expenditure per capita in Honduras, current prices, US$

The growth of government expenditure in Honduras, constant prices, 1970=100%

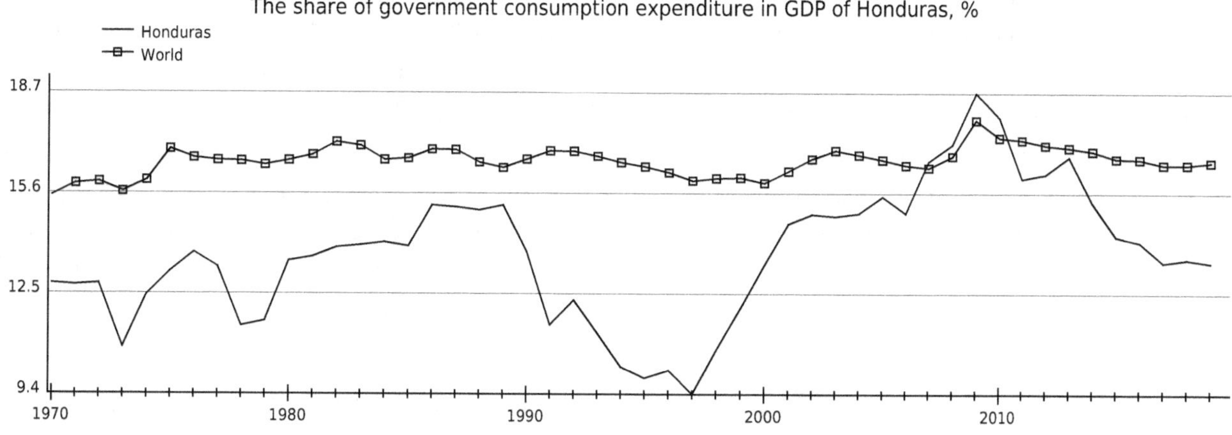

The 1970s

The Honduras government consumption expenditure was $185.8 million per year in the 1970s, ranked 103rd in the world, and was on a par with Niger ($185.9 million), Namibia ($184.0 million). The share in the world was 0.017%, and 0.051% in the Americas.

The share of public expenditure in GDP of Honduras was 12.5% in the 1970s, ranked 127th in the world, and was on a par with Belize (12.5%), Barbados (12.4%), China (12.4%).

The government expenditure per capita in Honduras was $59.6 in the 1970s, ranked 135th in the world, and was on a par with Madagascar ($60.5), Nicaragua ($58.4), Colombia ($58.3). The government consumption expenditure per capita in Honduras was less than public expenditure per capita in the world ($265.2) in 4.5 times, and was less than government expenditure per capita in the Americas ($655.5) in 11.0 times.

The growth of government expenditure in Honduras was 5.5% in the 1970s, ranked 89th in the world. The growth of government expenditure in Honduras (5.5%) was greater than growth of government expenditure in the world (3.7%), was greater than growth of public expenditure in the Americas (2.1%).

Comparison with neighbors. The government expenditure of Honduras was greater than in Nicaragua ($162.1 million) and in El Salvador ($75.7 million); but less than in Guatemala ($330.9 million). The government expenditure per capita in Honduras was greater than in Nicaragua ($58.4), in Guatemala ($52.1), and in El Salvador ($18.5). The growth of government expenditure in Honduras was greater than in Guatemala (5.2%); but less than in Nicaragua (9.6%) and in El Salvador (6.6%).

Comparison with leaders. The Honduran public expenditure was less than in the USA ($285.9 billion), in the USSR ($117.3 billion), in Germany ($95.6 billion), in Japan ($78.0 billion), and in France ($64.5 billion). The government consumption expenditure per capita in Honduras was less than in the USA ($1 310.2), in Germany ($1 213.7), in France ($1 202.3), in Japan ($700.2), and in the USSR ($465.0). The growth of government expenditure in Honduras was greater than in Japan (5.3%), in France (5.0%), in Germany (4.4%), and in the United States (0.94%); but less than in the USSR (7.2%).

The 1980s

The Honduras public expenditure was $625.7 million per year in the 1980s, ranked 95th in the world, and was on a par with Brunei ($630.4 million), Yemen ($638.7 million). The share in the world was 0.025%, and 0.073% in the Americas.

The share of government consumption expenditure in GDP of Honduras was 14.5% in the 1980s, ranked 121st in the world, and was on a par with Puerto Rico (14.6%), Brunei (14.6%).

The Honduran public expenditure per capita was $147.9 in the 1980s, ranked 124th in the world, and was on a par with Ivory Coast ($151.6). The government consumption expenditure per capita in Honduras was less than government consumption expenditure per capita in the world ($523.5) in 3.5 times, and was less than government consumption expenditure per capita in the Americas ($1 287.2) in 8.7 times.

The growth of public expenditure in Honduras was 4.3% in the 1980s, ranked 67th in the world. The growth of government consumption expenditure in Honduras (4.3%) was greater than growth of government expenditure in the world (2.7%), was greater than growth of government expenditure in the Americas (2.5%).

Comparison with neighbors. The public expenditure of Honduras was greater than in El Salvador ($304.2 million); but less than in Guatemala ($828.4 million) and in Nicaragua ($760.8 million). The public expenditure per capita in Honduras was greater than in Guatemala ($101.6) and in El Salvador ($62.1); but less than in Nicaragua ($206.7). The growth of public expenditure in Honduras was greater than in Guatemala (3.6%) and in El Salvador (1.8%); but less than in Nicaragua (4.9%).

Comparison with leaders. The government consumption expenditure of Honduras was less than in the United States ($665.3 billion), in Japan ($257.4 billion), in Germany ($203.7 billion), in the USSR ($181.1 billion), and in France ($159.8 billion). The public expenditure per capita in Honduras was less than in France ($2.8 thousand), in the United States ($2.8 thousand), in Germany ($2.6 thousand), in Japan ($2.1 thousand), and in the USSR ($658.0). The growth of government expenditure in Honduras was greater than in Japan (3.5%), in France (2.8%), in the USA (2.6%), and in Germany (0.98%); but less than in the USSR (5.4%).

The 1990s

The public expenditure of Honduras was $528.4 million per year in the 1990s, ranked 131st in the world, and was on a par with Mauritius ($517.4 million). The share in the world was 0.011%, and 0.035% in the Americas.

The share of government consumption expenditure in GDP of Honduras was 11.1% in the 1990s, ranked 166th in the world, and was on a par with Ecuador (11.1%), India (11.1%), Guyana (11.1%).

The government expenditure per capita in Honduras was $93.6 in the 1990s, ranked 159th in the world. The Honduras government expenditure per capita was less than government consumption expenditure per capita in the world ($824.8) in 8.8 times, and was less than public expenditure per capita in the Americas ($1 972.7) in 21.1 times.

The growth of government consumption expenditure in Honduras was -0.3% in the 1990s, ranked 155th in the world. The growth of government consumption expenditure in Honduras (-0.30%) was less than growth of public expenditure in the world (2.0%), was less than growth of public expenditure in the Americas (1.1%).

Comparison with neighbors. The public expenditure of Honduras was less than in Guatemala ($1.0 billion), in El Salvador ($864.9 million), and in Nicaragua ($572.2 million). The Honduras government consumption expenditure per capita was less than in El Salvador ($155.1), in Nicaragua ($124.5), and in Guatemala ($97.2). The growth of government expenditure in Honduras was greater than in Nicaragua (-1.1%); but less than in Guatemala (4.6%) and in El Salvador (2.5%).

Comparison with leaders. The government expenditure of Honduras was less than in the United States ($1.1 trillion), in Japan ($651.8 billion), in Germany ($419.6 billion), in France ($325.4 billion), and in the United Kingdom ($234.6 billion). The government consumption expenditure per capita in Honduras was less than in France ($5.5 thousand), in Germany ($5.2 thousand), in Japan ($5.2 thousand), in the United States ($4.3 thousand), and in the UK ($4.1 thousand). The growth of government expenditure in Honduras was less than in Japan (3.0%), in Germany (2.4%), in the UK (2.1%), in France (1.8%), and in the USA (1.3%).

The 2000s

The government expenditure of Honduras was $1.6 billion per year in the 2000s, ranked 107th in the world, and was on a par with Jamaica ($1.6 billion), Bolivia ($1.6 billion). The share in the world was 0.021%, and 0.063% in the Americas.

The share of government consumption expenditure in GDP of Honduras was 15.9% in the 2000s, ranked 98th in the world, and was on a par with Moldova (16.0%), South America (16.0%), Eastern Asia (16.0%).

The government expenditure per capita in Honduras was $219.0 in the 2000s, ranked 147th in the world. The Honduran government expenditure per capita was less than government expenditure per capita in the world ($1 200.9) in 5.5 times, and was less than public expenditure per capita in the Americas ($2 931.6) in 13.4 times.

The growth of public expenditure in Honduras was 7.2% in the 2000s, ranked 41st in the world, and was on a par with Malawi (7.2%), Vietnam (7.2%). The growth of government consumption expenditure in Honduras (7.2%) was greater than growth of government expenditure in the world (3.1%), was greater than growth of government consumption expenditure in the Americas (2.4%).

Comparison with neighbors. The Honduras government consumption expenditure was greater than in Nicaragua ($932.5 million); but less than in Guatemala ($2.6 billion) and in El Salvador ($2.1 billion). The Honduras government expenditure per capita was greater than in Guatemala ($201.6) and in Nicaragua ($172.5); but less than in El Salvador ($348.2). The growth of government consumption expenditure in Honduras was greater than in Guatemala (4.5%), in Nicaragua (2.5%), and in El Salvador (1.6%).

Comparison with leaders. The government expenditure of Honduras was less than in the USA ($1.9 trillion), in Japan ($844.2 billion), in Germany ($520.1 billion), in France ($479.9 billion), and in the United Kingdom ($453.4 billion). The Honduran government consumption expenditure per capita was less than in France ($7.6 thousand), in the UK ($7.5 thousand), in Japan ($6.6 thousand), in the United States ($6.5 thousand), and in Germany ($6.4 thousand). The growth of government expenditure in Honduras was greater than in the UK (2.9%), in the USA (2.2%), in Japan (1.7%), in France (1.7%), and in Germany (1.4%).

The 2010s

The government expenditure of Honduras was $3.1 billion per year in the 2010s, ranked 117th in the world, and was on a par with Zambia ($3.1 billion), Botswana ($3.0 billion). The share in the world was 0.023%, and 0.078% in the Americas.

The share of government expenditure in GDP of Honduras was 14.9% in the 2010s, ranked 123rd in the world, and was on a par with Madagascar (14.9%).

The government expenditure per capita in Honduras was $339.3 in the 2010s, ranked 155th in the world, and was on a par with Indonesia ($336.0), Moldova ($346.6). The government expenditure per capita in Honduras was less than government consumption expenditure per capita in the world ($1 785.1) in 5.3 times, and was less than government expenditure per capita in the Americas ($4 034.3) in 11.9 times.

The growth of government expenditure in Honduras was 1.1% in the 2010s, ranked 145th in the world. The growth of public expenditure in Honduras (1.1%) was less than growth of government expenditure in the world (2.3%), was greater than growth of government consumption expenditure in the Americas (0.45%).

Comparison with neighbors. The public expenditure of Honduras was 81.9% higher than in Nicaragua ($1.7 billion); but 2.1 times lower than in Guatemala ($6.6 billion) and 17.1% lower than in El Salvador ($3.7 billion). The Honduran government consumption expenditure per capita was 24.5% higher than in Nicaragua ($272.4); but 42.1% lower than in El Salvador ($585.6) and 16.7% lower than in Guatemala ($407.1). The growth of government expenditure in Honduras was less than in Nicaragua (3.6%), in Guatemala (3.6%), and in El Salvador (1.3%).

Comparison with leaders. The Honduras government consumption expenditure was 865.6 times lower than in the USA ($2.7 trillion), 547.8 times lower than in China ($1.7 trillion), 340.3 times lower than in Japan ($1.0 trillion), 235.4 times lower than in Germany ($721.6 billion), and 208.1 times lower than in France ($637.9 billion). The Honduras public expenditure per capita was 28.3 times lower than in France ($9.6 thousand), 26.0 times lower than in Germany ($8.8 thousand), 24.5 times lower than in the USA ($8.3 thousand), 24.0 times lower than in Japan ($8.2 thousand), and 3.5 times lower than in China ($1 197.3). The growth of government expenditure in Honduras was greater than in the United States (0.0052%); but less than in China (8.3%), in Germany (1.9%), in Japan (1.3%), and in France (1.3%).

Chapter XIII. Household consumption expenditure

(including Non-profit institutions serving households)

The Honduras household consumption expenditure grew up from $1.1 billion per year in the 1970s to $16.2 billion per year in the 2010s, that is by $15.1 billion or 15.3 times. The change occurred at $11.6 billion due to a 3.5-fold increase in prices, as also at $1.5 billion due to a 1.5-fold increase in per capita rate, as well as at $2.0 billion due to the rise in population. The average annual growth in household consumption expenditure is 3.9%. The minimum value of household expenditure was in 1970 at $603.1 million. The maximum value of household consumption expenditure was in 2019 at $20.2 billion.

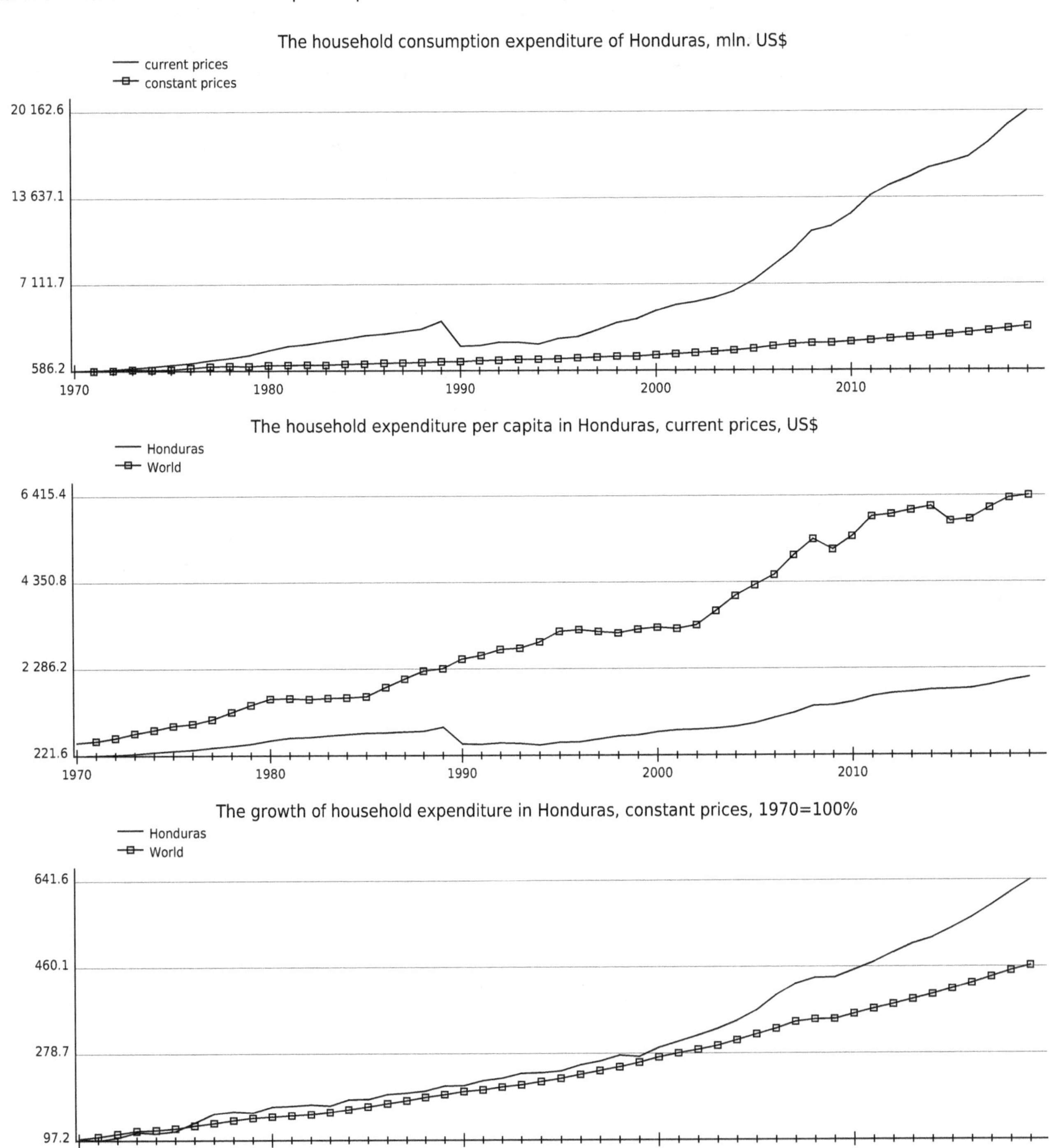

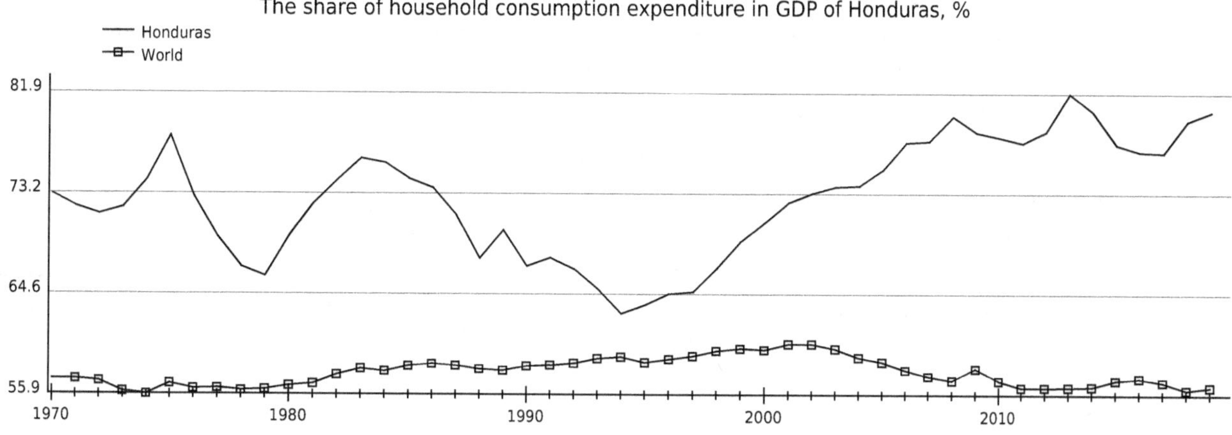

The 1970s

The Honduras household expenditure was $1.1 billion per year in the 1970s, ranked 101st in the world. The share in the world was 0.029%, and 0.076% in the Americas.

The share of household consumption expenditure in GDP of Honduras was 70.7% in the 1970s, ranked 64th in the world, and was on a par with Guyana (70.6%), Southern Asia (70.6%), Central America (70.6%).

The Honduran household consumption expenditure per capita was $337.8 in the 1970s, ranked 128th in the world, and was on a par with Grenada ($333.2), Cameroon ($343.1). The Honduras household expenditure per capita was less than household consumption expenditure per capita in the world ($914.8) in 2.7 times, and was less than household consumption expenditure per capita in the Americas ($2 467.5) in 7.3 times.

The growth of household consumption expenditure in Honduras was 5% in the 1970s, ranked 70th in the world, and was on a par with Turkey (5.0%), Costa Rica (5.0%), Sri Lanka (5.0%). The growth of household expenditure in Honduras (5.0%) was greater than growth of household expenditure in the world (4.1%), was greater than growth of household expenditure in the Americas (4.1%).

Comparison with neighbors. The Honduran household expenditure was greater than in El Salvador ($462.3 million); but less than in Guatemala ($2.5 billion) and in Nicaragua ($1.4 billion). The household expenditure per capita in Honduras was greater than in El Salvador ($112.7); but less than in Nicaragua ($514.7) and in Guatemala ($399.3). The growth of household consumption expenditure in Honduras was greater than in El Salvador (4.0%) and in Nicaragua (-0.35%); but less than in Guatemala (5.4%).

Comparison with leaders. The household consumption expenditure of Honduras was less than in the USA ($1.0 trillion), in the USSR ($310.6 billion), in Japan ($280.9 billion), in Germany ($277.8 billion), and in France ($180.7 billion). The Honduras household consumption expenditure per capita was less than in the USA ($4.7 thousand), in Germany ($3.5 thousand), in France ($3.4 thousand), in Japan ($2.5 thousand), and in the USSR ($1 231.6). The growth of household consumption expenditure in Honduras was greater than in the USSR (4.7%), in France (4.0%), in the USA (3.6%), and in Germany (3.6%); but less than in Japan (5.1%).

The 1980s

The household expenditure of Honduras was $3.1 billion per year in the 1980s, ranked 91st in the world. The share in the world was 0.036%, and 0.092% in the Americas.

The share of household expenditure in GDP of Honduras was 72.3% in the 1980s, ranked 61st in the world, and was on a par with Puerto Rico (72.4%), the Dominican Republic (72.1%), Niger (72.5%).

The household consumption expenditure per capita in Honduras was $735.8 in the 1980s, ranked 113th in the world, and was on a par with Palestine ($743.9), Guatemala ($748.0), Cameroon ($720.1). The Honduras household consumption expenditure per capita was less than household expenditure per capita in the world ($1 808.0) in 2.5 times, and was less than household expenditure per capita in the Americas ($5 090.2) in 6.9 times.

The growth of household expenditure in Honduras was 3.1% in the 1980s, ranked 80th in the world, and was on a par with DR Congo (3.1%), Middle Africa (3.1%). The growth of household consumption expenditure in Honduras (3.1%) was greater than growth of household consumption expenditure in the world (3.0%), was greater than growth of household consumption expenditure in the Americas (2.9%).

Comparison with neighbors. The household expenditure of Honduras was greater than in Nicaragua ($2.0 billion) and in El Salvador ($1.7 billion); but less than in Guatemala ($6.1 billion). The household consumption expenditure per capita in Honduras was greater than in Nicaragua ($544.0) and in El Salvador ($354.2); but less than in Guatemala ($748.0). The growth of household consumption expenditure in Honduras was greater than in Guatemala (1.3%), in Nicaragua (-1.3%), and in El Salvador (-1.5%).

Comparison with leaders. The household consumption expenditure of Honduras was less than in the United States ($2.6 trillion), in Japan ($945.6 billion), in Germany ($575.7 billion), in the USSR ($424.6 billion), and in the United Kingdom ($416.5 billion). The Honduran household consumption expenditure per capita was less than in the United States ($10.9 thousand), in Japan ($7.8 thousand), in Germany ($7.4 thousand), in the UK ($7.4 thousand), and in the USSR ($1 542.8). The growth of household expenditure in Honduras was greater than in the USSR (3.0%) and in Germany (1.8%); but less than in Japan (3.7%), in the UK (3.5%), and in the United States (3.2%).

The 1990s

The Honduran household consumption expenditure was $3.1 billion per year in the 1990s, ranked 114th in the world, and was on a par with Trinidad and Tobago ($3.1 billion), Azerbaijan ($3.1 billion). The share in the world was 0.019%, and 0.048% in the Americas.

The share of household consumption expenditure in GDP of Honduras was 65.9% in the 1990s, ranked 97th in the world, and was on a par with New Caledonia (65.8%), Jamaica (65.7%), Southern Asia (65.6%).

The household expenditure per capita in Honduras was $555.7 in the 1990s, ranked 151st in the world, and was on a par with Ivory Coast ($545.4), Cameroon ($566.9). The household consumption expenditure per capita in Honduras was less than household expenditure per capita in the world ($2 963.9) in 5.3 times, and was less than household expenditure per capita in the Americas ($8 394.4) in 15.1 times.

The growth of household expenditure in Honduras was 2.6% in the 1990s, ranked 111th in the world, and was on a par with Africa (2.6%), Libya (2.6%). The growth of household consumption expenditure in Honduras (2.6%) was less than growth of household expenditure in the world (3.0%), was less than growth of household consumption expenditure in the Americas (3.3%).

Comparison with neighbors. The household expenditure of Honduras was less than in Guatemala ($10.0 billion), in El Salvador ($6.9 billion), and in Nicaragua ($3.3 billion). The Honduras household expenditure per capita was less than in El Salvador ($1 241.7), in Guatemala ($973.3), and in Nicaragua ($712.6). The growth of household consumption expenditure in Honduras was less than in El Salvador (4.9%), in Nicaragua (4.3%), and in Guatemala (4.0%).

Comparison with leaders. The household consumption expenditure of Honduras was less than in the United States ($4.9 trillion), in Japan ($2.3 trillion), in Germany ($1.2 trillion), in the UK ($884.5 billion), and in France ($783.0 billion). The household expenditure per capita in Honduras was less than in the USA ($18.5 thousand), in Japan ($18.2 thousand), in the United Kingdom ($15.3 thousand), in Germany ($15.2 thousand), and in France ($13.2 thousand). The growth of household consumption expenditure in Honduras was greater than in Germany (2.1%), in Japan (1.8%), and in France (1.8%); but less than in the USA (3.4%) and in the UK (2.8%).

The 2000s

The household consumption expenditure of Honduras was $7.7 billion per year in the 2000s, ranked 106th in the world, and was on a par with Iceland ($7.7 billion). The share in the world was 0.028%, and 0.070% in the Americas.

The share of household expenditure in GDP of Honduras was 76.0% in the 2000s, ranked 54th in the world, and was on a par with Micronesia (76.0%), Chad (75.9%), Armenia (76.2%).

The household consumption expenditure per capita in Honduras was $1 045.5 in the 2000s, ranked 142nd in the world, and was on a par with South-Eastern Asia ($1 044.6), Syria ($1 044.6), Algeria ($1 059.4). The household consumption expenditure per capita in Honduras was less than household expenditure per capita in the world ($4 208.2) in 4.0 times, and was less than household consumption expenditure per capita in the Americas ($12 522.4) in 12.0 times.

The growth of household consumption expenditure in Honduras was 4.9% in the 2000s, ranked 73rd in the world, and was on a par with Montenegro (4.8%), Morocco (4.8%), Northern Africa (4.8%). The growth of household expenditure in Honduras (4.9%) was greater than growth of household expenditure in the world (3.0%), was greater than growth of household consumption expenditure in the Americas (2.7%).

Comparison with neighbors. The Honduran household consumption expenditure was greater than in Nicaragua ($5.2 billion); but less than in Guatemala ($22.7 billion) and in El Salvador ($12.8 billion). The Honduras household expenditure per capita was greater than in Nicaragua ($966.0); but less than in El Salvador ($2.1 thousand) and in Guatemala ($1 754.2). The growth of household expenditure in Honduras was greater than in Guatemala (3.7%), in Nicaragua (3.5%), and in El Salvador (2.1%).

Comparison with leaders. The Honduras household expenditure was less than in the United States ($8.5 trillion), in Japan ($2.6 trillion), in Germany ($1.5 trillion), in the United Kingdom ($1.5 trillion), and in France ($1.1 trillion). The household expenditure per capita in Honduras was less than in the United States ($28.8 thousand), in the UK ($25.0 thousand), in Japan ($20.4 thousand), in Germany ($18.9 thousand), and in France ($18.1 thousand). The growth of household expenditure in Honduras was greater than in the United States (2.4%), in the UK (2.1%), in France (2.0%), in Japan (0.81%), and in Germany (0.46%).

The 2010s

The Honduras household consumption expenditure was $16.2 billion per year in the 2010s, ranked 102nd in the world, and was on a par with Zimbabwe ($16.0 billion), Cyprus ($15.8 billion), Nepal ($16.6 billion). The share in the world was 0.037%, and 0.095% in the Americas.

The share of household consumption expenditure in GDP of Honduras was 78.8% in the 2010s, ranked 42nd in the world, and was on a par with Togo (78.8%), Micronesia (78.5%), Jordan (78.0%).

The Honduran household expenditure per capita was $1 790.2 in the 2010s, ranked 149th in the world, and was on a par with Morocco ($1 813.5), Algeria ($1 755.7). The Honduran household expenditure per capita was less than household expenditure per capita in the world ($6 018.5) in 3.4 times, and was less than household consumption expenditure per capita in the Americas ($17 389.9) in 9.7 times.

The growth of household expenditure in Honduras was 3.9% in the 2010s, ranked 77th in the world, and was on a par with Colombia (3.9%). The growth of household expenditure in Honduras (3.9%) was greater than growth of household expenditure in the world (2.8%), was greater than growth of household consumption expenditure in the Americas (2.2%).

Comparison with neighbors. The Honduran household consumption expenditure was 88.6% higher than in Nicaragua ($8.6 billion); but 3.1 times lower than in Guatemala ($50.8 billion) and 17.7% lower than in El Salvador ($19.7 billion). The Honduras household expenditure per capita was 29.1% higher than in Nicaragua ($1 386.6); but 43.3% lower than in Guatemala ($3.2 thousand) and 42.5% lower than in El Salvador ($3.1 thousand). The growth of household consumption expenditure in Honduras was greater than in Guatemala (3.9%), in Nicaragua (2.4%), and in El Salvador (2.2%).

Comparison with leaders. The household expenditure of Honduras was 753.9 times lower than in the United States ($12.2 trillion), 243.0 times lower than in China ($3.9 trillion), 184.7 times lower than in Japan ($3.0 trillion), 121.1 times lower than in Germany ($2.0 trillion), and 110.2 times lower than in the UK ($1.8 trillion). The household consumption expenditure per capita in Honduras was 21.3 times lower than in the USA ($38.2 thousand), 15.2 times lower than in the UK ($27.2 thousand), 13.4 times lower than in Germany ($23.9 thousand), 13.0 times lower than in Japan ($23.4 thousand), and 36.1% lower than in China ($2.8 thousand). The growth of household expenditure in Honduras was greater than in the USA (2.4%), in the United Kingdom (1.8%), in Germany (1.4%), and in Japan (0.64%); but less than in China (8.3%).

Chapter XIV. Food consumption

During the research period the food consumption grew in treenuts (in 17.5 times), fish (in 2.9 times), meat (in 2.9 times), vegetable oils (in 2.6 times), vegetables (in 2.6 times), spices (in 2.1 times), alcoholic beverages (by 62.5%), sugar (by 53.2%), pulses (by 31.5%), milk (by 28.5%), stimulants (by 22.6%), starchy roots (by 18.8%), eggs (by 11.3%), cereals (by 9.0%), but fell in fruits (by 11.7%).

These are the correlation coefficients between the GNI per capita in constant prices and the food consumption: cereals (0.995), alcoholic beverages (0.975), vegetables (0.974), sugar (0.968), pulses (0.966), meat (0.962), vegetable oils (0.9), spices (0.898), treenuts (0.89), fish (0.879), milk (0.718), starchy roots (0.594), stimulants (0.422), eggs (0.259), fruits (-0.584).

The 1970s

Kcal supply in Honduras was 2 053.2 kcal/capita/day in the 1970s, ranked 109th in the world, and was on a par with Eastern Asia (2 056.5 kcal/capita/day), Indonesia (2 063.0 kcal/capita/day), Niger (2 042.9 kcal/capita/day). Kcal supply in Honduras was less than in the world (2 403.2 kcal/capita/day), and was less than in the Americas (2 754.7 kcal/capita/day). Structure of kcal supply: cereals (54.8%), sugar (14.5%), fruits (7.5%), vegetable oils (5.1%), milk (4.8%), and others (13.3%).

Protein supply in Honduras was 51.3 g/capita/day in the 1970s, ranked 112th in the world, and was on a par with Southern Asia (51.3 g/capita/day), Gambia (51.5 g/capita/day), Saint Lucia (51.7 g/capita/day). Protein supply in Honduras was less than in the world (65.0 g/capita/day), and was less than in the Americas (79.0 g/capita/day). Structure of protein supply: cereals (56.6%), milk (13.8%), pulses (9.6%), meat (8.5%), fruits (3.5%), and others (8%).

Fat supply in Honduras was 41.2 g/capita/day in the 1970s, ranked 109th in the world, and was on a par with Chad (41.1 g/capita/day), Congo (41.3 g/capita/day). Fat supply in Honduras was less than in the world (55.1 g/capita/day), and was less than in the Americas (85.8 g/capita/day). Structure of fat supply: vegetable oils (29.1%), cereals (28.1%), milk (11.7%), meat (11.5%), eggs (2.6%), and others (17%).

These are the levels of food consumption in the world rankings: 38th - pulses (8.2 kg/capita/yr), 41st - fruits (91.1 kg/capita/yr), 44th - stimulants (2.8 kg/capita/yr), 60th - eggs (4.6 kg/capita/yr), 63rd - milk (74.2 kg/capita/yr), 71st - cereals (123.4 kg/capita/yr), 74th - sugar (30.6 kg/capita/yr), 100th - alcoholic beverages (12.5 kg/capita/yr), 103rd - vegetable oils (4.4 kg/capita/yr), 110th - meat (11.8 kg/capita/yr), 118th - spices (0.085 kg/capita/yr), 122nd - vegetables (19.1 kg/capita/yr), 137th - fish (1.3 kg/capita/yr), 138th - starchy roots (6.8 kg/capita/yr).

The 1980s

Kcal supply in Honduras was 2 143.3 kcal/capita/day in the 1980s, ranked 116th in the world, and was on a par with Peru (2 146.6 kcal/capita/day), DPRK (2 138.0 kcal/capita/day), Zimbabwe (2 131.5 kcal/capita/day). Kcal supply in Honduras was less than in the world (2 572.3 kcal/capita/day), and was less than in the Americas (2 917.7 kcal/capita/day). Structure of kcal supply: cereals (53%), sugar (14.6%), vegetable oils (7.9%), fruits (6.7%), milk (4.8%), and others (13%).

Protein supply in Honduras was 51.6 g/capita/day in the 1980s, ranked 119th in the world, and was on a par with Cameroon (51.3 g/capita/day), Nepal (51.3 g/capita/day), Gambia (52.1 g/capita/day). Protein supply in Honduras was less than in the world (69.1 g/capita/day), and was less than in the Americas (81.7 g/capita/day). Structure of protein supply: cereals (56.8%), milk (13.4%), pulses (9.6%), meat (9.2%), fruits (3.2%), and others (7.8%).

Fat supply in Honduras was 49.6 g/capita/day in the 1980s, ranked 95th in the world, and was on a par with Suriname (49.6 g/capita/day), Liberia (49.4 g/capita/day). Fat supply in Honduras was less than in the world (63.2 g/capita/day), and was less than in the Americas (96.3 g/capita/day). Structure of fat supply: vegetable oils (38.8%), cereals (23%), milk (10.4%), meat (9.8%), eggs (2.4%), and others (15.6%).

These are the levels of food consumption in the world rankings: 31st - pulses (8.2 kg/capita/yr), 45th - fruits (88.6 kg/capita/yr), 68th - sugar (32.1 kg/capita/yr), 70th - milk (73.2 kg/capita/yr), 71st - eggs (5.0 kg/capita/yr), 77th - cereals (125.5 kg/capita/yr), 90th - stimulants (1.2 kg/capita/yr), 93rd - vegetable oils (7.0 kg/capita/yr), 96th - alcoholic beverages (13.9 kg/capita/yr), 115th - meat (13.0 kg/capita/yr), 116th - treenuts (0.034 kg/capita/yr), 122nd - spices (0.092 kg/capita/yr), 133rd - fish (1.9 kg/capita/yr), 145th - starchy roots (4.5 kg/capita/yr).

The 1990s

Kcal supply in Honduras was 2 360.1 kcal/capita/day in the 1990s, ranked 110th in the world, and was on a par with Pakistan (2 362.8 kcal/capita/day), Cabo Verde (2 365.1 kcal/capita/day), Saint Vincent and the Grenadines (2 365.1 kcal/capita/day). Kcal supply in Honduras was less than in the world (2 652.6 kcal/capita/day), and was less than in the Americas (3 035.8 kcal/capita/day). Structure of kcal supply: cereals (48.1%), sugar (16.2%), vegetable oils (9.8%), milk (6.2%), fruits (5.5%), and others (14.2%).

Protein supply in Honduras was 57.6 g/capita/day in the 1990s, ranked 119th in the world, and was on a par with Kenya (57.5 g/capita/day), Guatemala (58.1 g/capita/day), Eswatini (58.2 g/capita/day). Protein supply in Honduras was less than in the world (72.1 g/capita/day), and was less than in the Americas (86.2 g/capita/day). Structure of protein supply: cereals (50.5%), milk (15.2%), meat (12.3%), pulses (9.9%), eggs (2.9%), and others (9.2%).

Fat supply in Honduras was 61.0 g/capita/day in the 1990s, ranked 100th in the world, and was on a par with Northern Africa (61.5 g/capita/day). Fat supply in Honduras was less than in the world (69.0 g/capita/day), and was less than in the Americas (100.9 g/capita/day). Structure of fat supply: vegetable oils (42.8%), cereals (18.3%), milk (12.4%), meat (10.6%), eggs (2.4%), and others (13.5%).

These are the levels of food consumption in the world rankings: 27th - pulses (9.4 kg/capita/yr), 37th - stimulants (4.8 kg/capita/yr), 47th - sugar (39.0 kg/capita/yr), 64th - fruits (81.7 kg/capita/yr), 69th - eggs (6.1 kg/capita/yr), 78th - milk (94.1 kg/capita/yr), 80th - vegetable oils (9.5 kg/capita/yr), 84th - cereals (126.3 kg/capita/yr), 104th - alcoholic beverages (16.6 kg/capita/yr), 112th - meat (19.2 kg/capita/yr), 125th - vegetables (33.7 kg/capita/yr), 136th - fish (3.3 kg/capita/yr), 168th - starchy roots (3.6 kg/capita/yr).

The 2000s

Kcal supply in Honduras was 2 504.5 kcal/capita/day in the 2000s, ranked 110th in the world, and was on a par with Gambia (2 507.0 kcal/capita/day), Africa (2 509.9 kcal/capita/day), Indonesia (2 487.0 kcal/capita/day). Kcal supply in Honduras was less than in the world (2 765.9 kcal/capita/day), and was less than in the Americas (3 186.4 kcal/capita/day). Structure of kcal supply: cereals (46.6%), sugar (16.1%), vegetable oils (10.4%), milk (6.9%), meat (5.5%), and others (14.5%).

Protein supply in Honduras was 63.8 g/capita/day in the 2000s, ranked 117th in the world, and was on a par with Vietnam (63.8 g/capita/day), Namibia (64.2 g/capita/day), Colombia (63.2 g/capita/day). Protein supply in Honduras was less than in the world (76.5 g/capita/day), and was less than in the Americas (91.2 g/capita/day). Structure of protein supply: cereals (46.1%), meat (17.4%), milk (16%), pulses (9.2%), eggs (2.4%), and others (8.9%).

Fat supply in Honduras was 69.9 g/capita/day in the 2000s, ranked 96th in the world, and was on a par with Mauritania (69.7 g/capita/day), Iran (69.7 g/capita/day), Belize (69.2 g/capita/day). Fat supply in Honduras was less than in the world (76.9 g/capita/day), and was less than in the Americas (113.5 g/capita/day). Structure of fat supply: vegetable oils (42.1%), cereals (16.1%), meat (14.4%), milk (12.9%), eggs (1.9%), and others (12.6%).

These are the levels of food consumption in the world rankings: 34th - pulses (9.7 kg/capita/yr), 41st - sugar (42.8 kg/capita/yr), 55th - stimulants (4.7 kg/capita/yr), 72nd - milk (110.6 kg/capita/yr), 81st - vegetable oils (10.8 kg/capita/yr), 83rd - eggs (5.6 kg/capita/yr), 84th - cereals (129.9 kg/capita/yr), 97th - fruits (66.1 kg/capita/yr), 102nd - meat (31.6 kg/capita/yr), 114th - alcoholic beverages (18.2 kg/capita/yr), 126th - vegetables (43.3 kg/capita/yr), 132nd - treenuts (0.30 kg/capita/yr), 135th - spices (0.19 kg/capita/yr), 150th - fish (3.4 kg/capita/yr), 172nd - starchy roots (7.2 kg/capita/yr).

The 2010s

Kcal supply in Honduras was 2 622.5 kcal/capita/day in the 2010s, ranked 114th in the world, and was on a par with Nepal (2 625.5 kcal/capita/day), the Bahamas (2 626.8 kcal/capita/day), Africa (2 612.5 kcal/capita/day). Kcal supply in Honduras was less than in the world (2 869.3 kcal/capita/day), and was less than in the Americas (3 219.3 kcal/capita/day). Structure of kcal supply: cereals (45.8%), sugar (16.9%), vegetable oils (10.6%), milk (5.7%), meat (5.6%), and others (15.4%).

Protein supply in Honduras was 64.5 g/capita/day in the 2010s, ranked 126th in the world, and was on a par with Botswana (64.5 g/capita/day), Cambodia (64.5 g/capita/day), Pakistan (64.5 g/capita/day). Protein supply in Honduras was less than in the world (80.6 g/capita/day), and was less than in the Americas (92.7 g/capita/day). Structure of protein supply: cereals (46.9%), meat (17.8%), milk (13.7%), pulses (10.1%), eggs (2.1%), and others (9.4%).

Fat supply in Honduras was 72.0 g/capita/day in the 2010s, ranked 105th in the world, and was on a par with Asia (72.1 g/capita/day). Fat supply in Honduras was less than in the world (82.4 g/capita/day), and was less than in the Americas (118.2 g/capita/day).

Structure of fat supply: vegetable oils (43.7%), cereals (16.7%), meat (15.2%), milk (10.8%), eggs (1.7%), and others (11.9%).

These are the levels of food consumption in the world rankings: 30th - sugar (46.8 kg/capita/yr), 33rd - pulses (10.7 kg/capita/yr), 80th - fruits (81.6 kg/capita/yr), 82nd - cereals (134.4 kg/capita/yr), 83rd - stimulants (3.4 kg/capita/yr), 88th - milk (95.4 kg/capita/yr), 95th - eggs (5.1 kg/capita/yr), 107th - meat (33.7 kg/capita/yr), 113th - alcoholic beverages (20.3 kg/capita/yr), 119th - vegetables (49.3 kg/capita/yr), 129th - treenuts (0.40 kg/capita/yr), 138th - spices (0.18 kg/capita/yr), 149th - fish (3.8 kg/capita/yr), 172nd - starchy roots (8.1 kg/capita/yr).

Part V. Reproduction

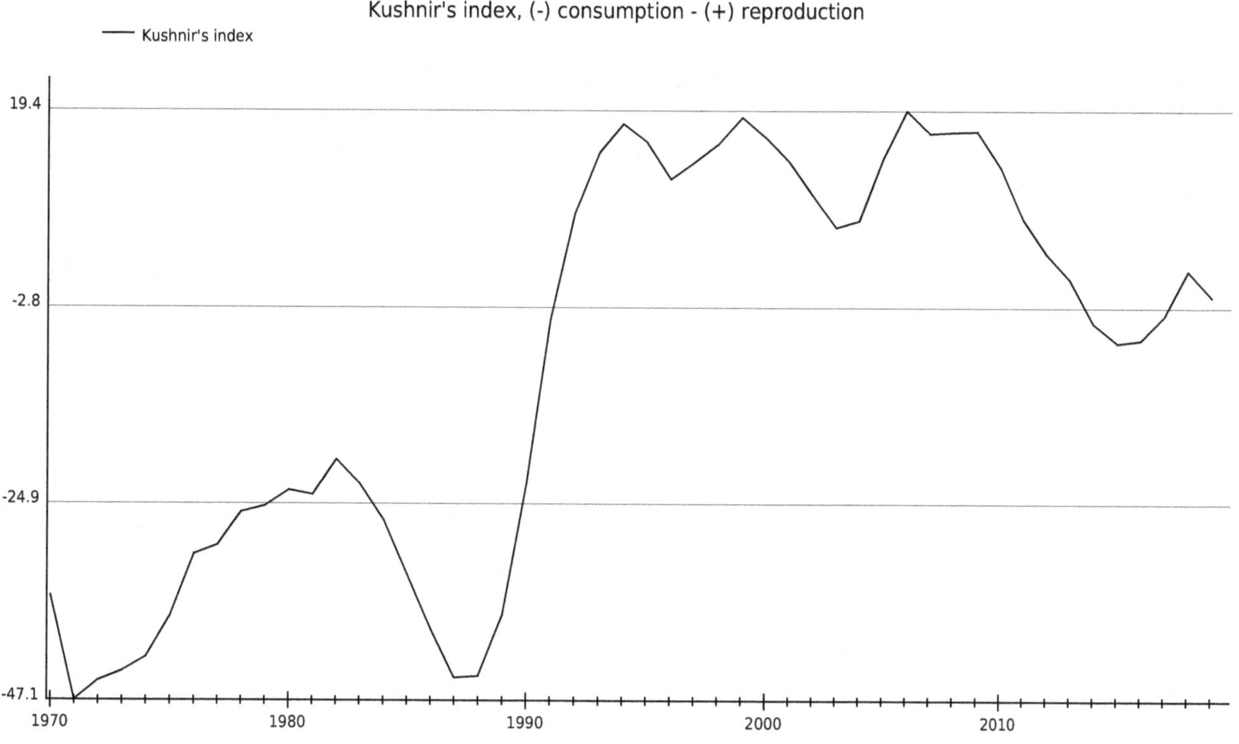

Chapter XV. Gross fixed capital formation

(including Acquisitions less disposals of valuables)

The Honduras gross fixed capital formation increased from $307.5 million per year in the 1970s to $4.8 billion per year in the 2010s, that is by $4.5 billion or 15.5 times. The change occurred at $3.6 billion due to a 4.0-fold increase in prices, as also at $314.3 million due to a 1.4-fold increase in per capita rate, as well as at $582.8 million due to the rise in population. The average annual growth in gross fixed capital formation is 3.6%. The minimum value of fixed capital formation was in 1972 at $144.1 million. The maximum value of gross fixed capital formation was in 2018 at $5.8 billion.

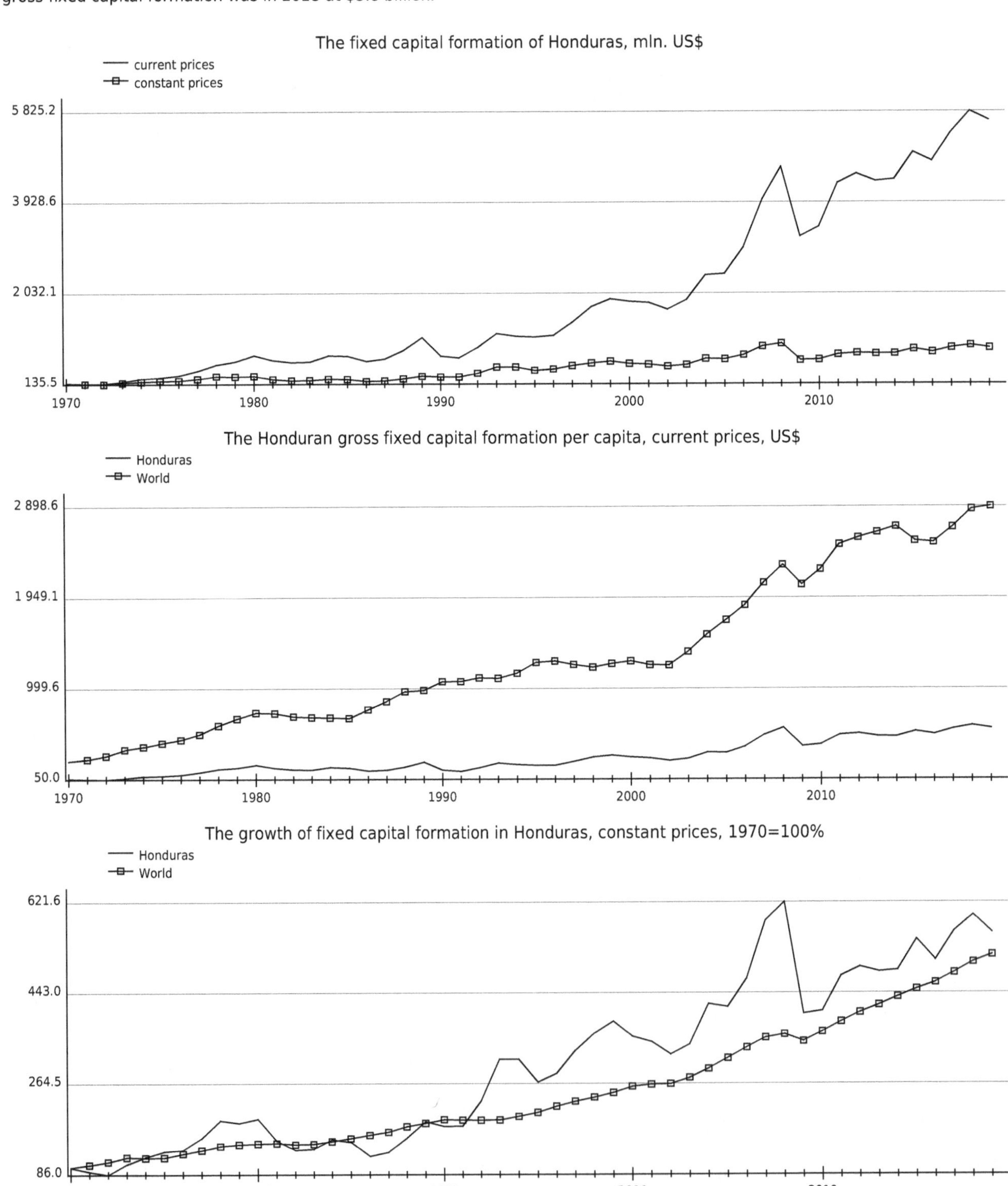

The fixed capital formation of Honduras, mln. US$

The Honduran gross fixed capital formation per capita, current prices, US$

The growth of fixed capital formation in Honduras, constant prices, 1970=100%

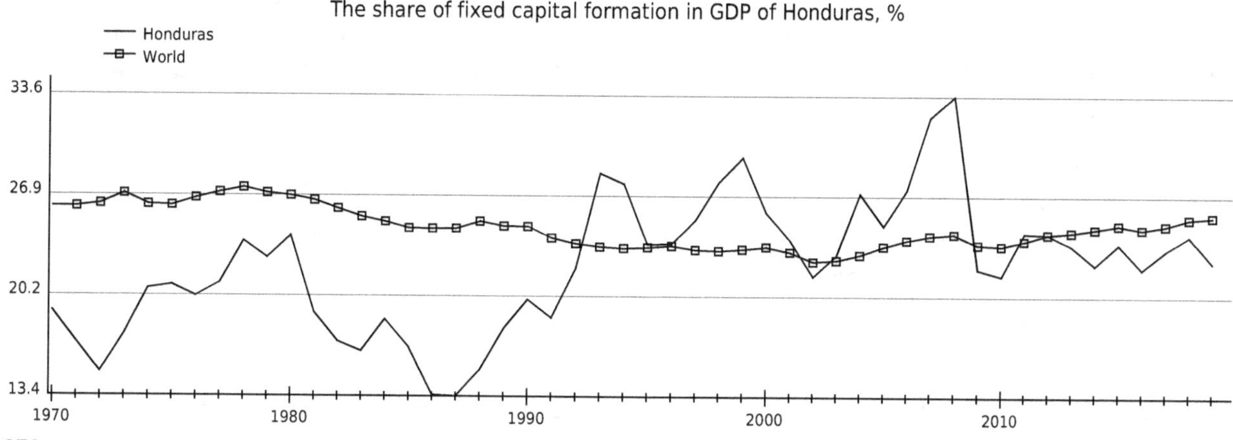

The 1970s

The Honduras fixed capital formation was $307.5 million per year in the 1970s, ranked 102nd in the world. The share in the world was 0.018%, and 0.060% in the Americas.

The share of gross fixed capital formation in GDP of Honduras was 20.6% in the 1970s, ranked 114th in the world, and was on a par with Saint Kitts and Nevis (20.5%), Puerto Rico (20.5%).

The fixed capital formation per capita in Honduras was $98.6 in the 1970s, ranked 131st in the world, and was on a par with Saint Vincent and the Grenadines ($98.6), Dominica ($98.1), Guinea-Bissau ($97.8). The Honduras fixed capital formation per capita was less than fixed capital formation per capita in the world ($433.5) in 4.4 times, and was less than gross fixed capital formation per capita in the Americas ($913.4) in 9.3 times.

The growth of fixed capital formation in Honduras was 7.2% in the 1970s, ranked 74th in the world, and was on a par with Botswana (7.3%). The growth of gross fixed capital formation in Honduras (7.2%) was greater than growth of fixed capital formation in the world (4.2%), was greater than growth of gross fixed capital formation in the Americas (5.3%).

Comparison with neighbors. The fixed capital formation of Honduras was greater than in Nicaragua ($288.1 million) and in El Salvador ($121.6 million); but less than in Guatemala ($727.3 million). The Honduran gross fixed capital formation per capita was greater than in El Salvador ($29.6); but less than in Guatemala ($114.5) and in Nicaragua ($103.8). The growth of fixed capital formation in Honduras was greater than in Nicaragua (-10.5%); but less than in El Salvador (9.5%) and in Guatemala (7.8%).

Comparison with leaders. The Honduras fixed capital formation was less than in the United States ($381.9 billion), in the USSR ($214.6 billion), in Japan ($191.6 billion), in Germany ($125.8 billion), and in France ($82.9 billion). The gross fixed capital formation per capita in Honduras was less than in the United States ($1 750.0), in Japan ($1 720.7), in Germany ($1 597.2), in France ($1 545.4), and in the USSR ($850.9). The growth of fixed capital formation in Honduras was greater than in the USA (4.4%), in Japan (3.9%), in the USSR (3.2%), in France (2.7%), and in Germany (1.5%).

The 1980s

The gross fixed capital formation of Honduras was $726.7 million per year in the 1980s, ranked 95th in the world, and was on a par with French Polynesia ($725.6 million), Lebanon ($723.4 million). The share in the world was 0.019%, and 0.059% in the Americas.

The share of fixed capital formation in GDP of Honduras was 16.9% in the 1980s, ranked 141st in the world, and was on a par with Jamaica (16.9%).

The Honduran fixed capital formation per capita was $171.8 in the 1980s, ranked 128th in the world, and was on a par with the Maldives ($173.7), Guyana ($168.2), the Philippines ($176.2). The Honduras fixed capital formation per capita was less than gross fixed capital formation per capita in the world ($790.9) in 4.6 times, and was less than fixed capital formation per capita in the Americas ($1 848.1) in 10.8 times.

The growth of fixed capital formation in Honduras was 0.1% in the 1980s, ranked 123rd in the world. The growth of fixed capital formation in Honduras (0.13%) was less than growth of gross fixed capital formation in the world (2.5%), was less than growth of fixed capital formation in the Americas (1.9%).

Comparison with neighbors. The Honduras gross fixed capital formation was greater than in Nicaragua ($499.0 million) and in El Salvador ($279.6 million); but less than in Guatemala ($1.2 billion). The gross fixed capital formation per capita in Honduras was greater than in Guatemala ($149.3), in Nicaragua ($135.6), and in El Salvador ($57.0). The growth of gross fixed capital formation in Honduras was greater than in El Salvador (-2.2%) and in Guatemala (-2.6%); but less than in Nicaragua (9.2%).

Comparison with leaders. The Honduras gross fixed capital formation was less than in the USA ($958.4 billion), in Japan ($571.7 billion), in the USSR ($271.0 billion), in Germany ($238.1 billion), and in France ($164.3 billion). The Honduras gross fixed capital formation per capita was less than in Japan ($4.7 thousand), in the USA ($4.0 thousand), in Germany ($3.1 thousand), in France ($2.9 thousand), and in the USSR ($984.8). The growth of fixed capital formation in Honduras was less than in Japan (4.8%), in the United States (3.1%), in France (2.4%), in the USSR (1.7%), and in Germany (1.4%).

The 1990s

The fixed capital formation of Honduras was $1.2 billion per year in the 1990s, ranked 106th in the world, and was on a par with Senegal ($1.2 billion), Ethiopia ($1.2 billion), Uganda ($1.2 billion). The share in the world was 0.018%, and 0.058% in the Americas.

The share of fixed capital formation in GDP of Honduras was 25.1% in the 1990s, ranked 59th in the world, and was on a par with Portugal (25.1%), Qatar (25.1%), Mauritius (25.2%).

The fixed capital formation per capita in Honduras was $212.0 in the 1990s, ranked 147th in the world, and was on a par with Bulgaria ($215.9). The Honduran gross fixed capital formation per capita was less than gross fixed capital formation per capita in the world ($1 183.8) in 5.6 times, and was less than gross fixed capital formation per capita in the Americas ($2 694.1) in 12.7 times.

The growth of gross fixed capital formation in Honduras was 7.4% in the 1990s, ranked 33rd in the world, and was on a par with Qatar (7.3%), Mozambique (7.4%), Argentina (7.4%). The growth of fixed capital formation in Honduras (7.4%) was greater than growth of fixed capital formation in the world (2.8%), was greater than growth of gross fixed capital formation in the Americas (4.4%).

Comparison with neighbors. The fixed capital formation of Honduras was greater than in Nicaragua ($765.6 million); but less than in Guatemala ($2.3 billion) and in El Salvador ($1.4 billion). The fixed capital formation per capita in Honduras was greater than in Nicaragua ($166.6); but less than in El Salvador ($247.7) and in Guatemala ($222.9). The growth of gross fixed capital formation in Honduras was greater than in El Salvador (5.7%); but less than in Nicaragua (7.6%) and in Guatemala (7.4%).

Comparison with leaders. The Honduras fixed capital formation was less than in the United States ($1.6 trillion), in Japan ($1.3 trillion), in Germany ($520.7 billion), in France ($299.3 billion), and in the United Kingdom ($250.0 billion). The Honduran fixed capital formation per capita was less than in Japan ($10.4 thousand), in Germany ($6.5 thousand), in the USA ($6.1 thousand), in France ($5.0 thousand), and in the United Kingdom ($4.3 thousand). The growth of gross fixed capital formation in Honduras was greater than in the USA (4.8%), in Germany (2.4%), in the UK (1.7%), in France (1.5%), and in Japan (0.18%).

The 2000s

The fixed capital formation of Honduras was $2.7 billion per year in the 2000s, ranked 106th in the world, and was on a par with Albania ($2.7 billion), Equatorial Guinea ($2.8 billion). The share in the world was 0.024%, and 0.075% in the Americas.

The share of gross fixed capital formation in GDP of Honduras was 26.6% in the 2000s, ranked 59th in the world, and was on a par with the Bahamas (26.6%), Switzerland (26.6%), Australasia (26.5%).

The Honduras fixed capital formation per capita was $365.5 in the 2000s, ranked 145th in the world, and was on a par with Indonesia ($356.7). The Honduras fixed capital formation per capita was less than fixed capital formation per capita in the world ($1 690.7) in 4.6 times, and was less than fixed capital formation per capita in the Americas ($4 079.3) in 11.2 times.

The growth of fixed capital formation in Honduras was 0.4% in the 2000s, ranked 182nd in the world. The growth of gross fixed capital formation in Honduras (0.38%) was less than growth of gross fixed capital formation in the world (3.5%), was less than growth of fixed capital formation in the Americas (1.3%).

Comparison with neighbors. The Honduran fixed capital formation was greater than in El Salvador ($2.5 billion) and in Nicaragua ($1.5 billion); but less than in Guatemala ($5.2 billion). The gross fixed capital formation per capita in Honduras was greater than in Nicaragua ($276.0); but less than in El Salvador ($419.8) and in Guatemala ($399.4). The growth of gross fixed capital formation in Honduras was greater than in El Salvador (0.11%), in Guatemala (0.067%), and in Nicaragua (-1.3%).

Comparison with leaders. The gross fixed capital formation of Honduras was less than in the USA ($2.8 trillion), in Japan ($1.2 trillion), in China ($1.0 trillion), in Germany ($557.7 billion), and in France ($463.9 billion). The fixed capital formation per capita in Honduras was less than in the United States ($9.4 thousand), in Japan ($9.0 thousand), in France ($7.4 thousand), in Germany ($6.9 thousand), and in China ($782.2). The growth of fixed capital formation in Honduras was greater than in Germany (-0.56%) and in Japan (-2.0%); but less than in China (13.4%), in France (1.6%), and in the USA (0.43%).

The 2010s

The fixed capital formation of Honduras was $4.8 billion per year in the 2010s, ranked 112th in the world, and was on a par with Senegal ($4.8 billion), Yemen ($4.7 billion), Equatorial Guinea ($4.9 billion). The share in the world was 0.025%, and 0.092% in the Americas.

The share of gross fixed capital formation in GDP of Honduras was 23.2% in the 2010s, ranked 97th in the world, and was on a par with Japan (23.1%), Azerbaijan (23.3%), Cameroon (23.1%).

The Honduran gross fixed capital formation per capita was $527.2 in the 2010s, ranked 154th in the world, and was on a par with India ($535.2), Mauritania ($535.3), Uzbekistan ($535.7). The Honduran fixed capital formation per capita was less than gross fixed capital formation per capita in the world ($2 621.1) in 5.0 times, and was less than fixed capital formation per capita in the Americas ($5 284.2) in 10.0 times.

The growth of fixed capital formation in Honduras was 3.4% in the 2010s, ranked 98th in the world, and was on a par with Saudi Arabia (3.4%), Ecuador (3.4%), Sweden (3.4%). The growth of gross fixed capital formation in Honduras (3.4%) was less than growth of gross fixed capital formation in the world (4.1%), was greater than growth of fixed capital formation in the Americas (2.9%).

Comparison with neighbors. The gross fixed capital formation of Honduras was 26.6% higher than in El Salvador ($3.8 billion) and 59.5% higher than in Nicaragua ($3.0 billion); but 45.4% lower than in Guatemala ($8.7 billion). The Honduran gross fixed capital formation per capita was 9.2% higher than in Nicaragua ($482.9); but 11.6% lower than in El Salvador ($596.0) and 2.7% lower than in Guatemala ($541.7). The growth of gross fixed capital formation in Honduras was greater than in Guatemala (2.7%) and in Nicaragua (2.1%); but less than in El Salvador (4.9%).

Comparison with leaders. The Honduran gross fixed capital formation was 949.6 times lower than in China ($4.5 trillion), 755.7 times lower than in the USA ($3.6 trillion), 254.1 times lower than in Japan ($1.2 trillion), 158.0 times lower than in Germany ($752.5 billion), and 146.3 times lower than in India ($696.8 billion). The gross fixed capital formation per capita in Honduras was 21.4 times lower than in the USA ($11.3 thousand), 17.9 times lower than in Japan ($9.5 thousand), 17.4 times lower than in Germany ($9.2 thousand), 6.1 times lower than in China ($3.2 thousand), and 1.5% lower than in India ($535.2). The growth of gross fixed capital formation in Honduras was greater than in Germany (2.8%) and in Japan (1.8%); but less than in China (8.0%), in India (5.8%), and in the United States (3.8%).